The Survival Guide Series

on

Basic Concepts of Saving and Investing

YOUR PERSONAL SURVIVAL GUIDE

ON

PROTECTION

NOTEBOOK AND INFORMATION GUIDE

Presented by:
The Successful Retirement Planning Institute

Published by The Successful Retirement Planning Institute, Inc.
50 N. Brockway, Suite 4-1
Palatine, Illinois 60067-5076

NOTICE OF DISCLAIMER

This video and notebook are meant to be an educational overview of the retirement planning process. It is not an investment product sales presentation. The Successful Retirement Planning Institute does not sell or recommend investment products or services nor does it receive compensation of any kind from anyone for the promotion of their products or services. Because of this independence, this video seminar can be as objective as possible in the discussion of investments and every aspect of planning for your retirement.

Although the retirement planning process is explained in detail throughout this video and notebook, this presentation is not meant to direct any individual plan. It should not be concluded that any specific plan is advocated by this presentation. Each individual is unique and must develop his or her own individual plan. Every individual has their own financial goals, needs and risk tolerance.

Information contained in this video and notebook may not apply to cases involving specific individuals. Users are advised that no privity of contract is created between the author of this work and any user or purchaser, and the author, publisher, and producer make no representations as to the applicability of any information contained herein to the circumstances of any user or purchaser.

During this presentation, investments will be mentioned and explained but this is not meant, in any way, to be an endorsement or a guarantee of performance of these investments. In addition, any investment should be analyzed for suitability for the individual as to how it fits into the individual's plan for financial independence.

This video and notebook are designed to provide accurate, up-to-date, authoritative information. The Successful Retirement Planning Institute is not engaged in rendering legal, accounting, tax, brokerage, or investment advice. If such assistance is required, the services of a competent professional should be sought.

QUALITY GUARANTEE

It is our goal to provide you with the best quality seminar and support materials. If you encounter any defects in the audio or video portions of this seminar or in the printed copy in your notebook, please contact The Successful Retirement Planning Institute at **(708) 359-1777** immediately so that we may be able to correct the problem.

SPECIAL ARRANGEMENTS

Successful Retirement Planning Institute video seminars and notebooks are available at special discounts for bulk purchases for sales promotions, premiums, fund-raising or educational use. Special edition or excerpts can also be created to specification for shorten versions of any part of the seminar. For details contact: Sales Director, The Successful Retirement Planning Institute, Inc., 50 N. Brockway, Suite 4-1, Palatine, Illinois 60067-5076 **(708) 359-1777**.

DEDICATION

THE SUCCESSFUL RETIREMENT PLANNING INSTITUTE DEDICATES THIS SEMINAR TO YOU AND YOUR SUCCESS IN RETIREMENT PLANNING.

REMEMBER, NO ONE WILL DO IT FOR YOU. IT IS UP TO YOU TO START PLANNING TODAY. YOU DESERVE TO BE SUCCESSFUL. INVEST YOUR TIME WISELY AND PLAN FOR YOUR RETIREMENT.

Your Personal Survival Guide on

Protection

Notebook Index

Your Personal Survival Guide on

Protection

Index of Topics by Tape Counter

PROTECTION FLOW CHART

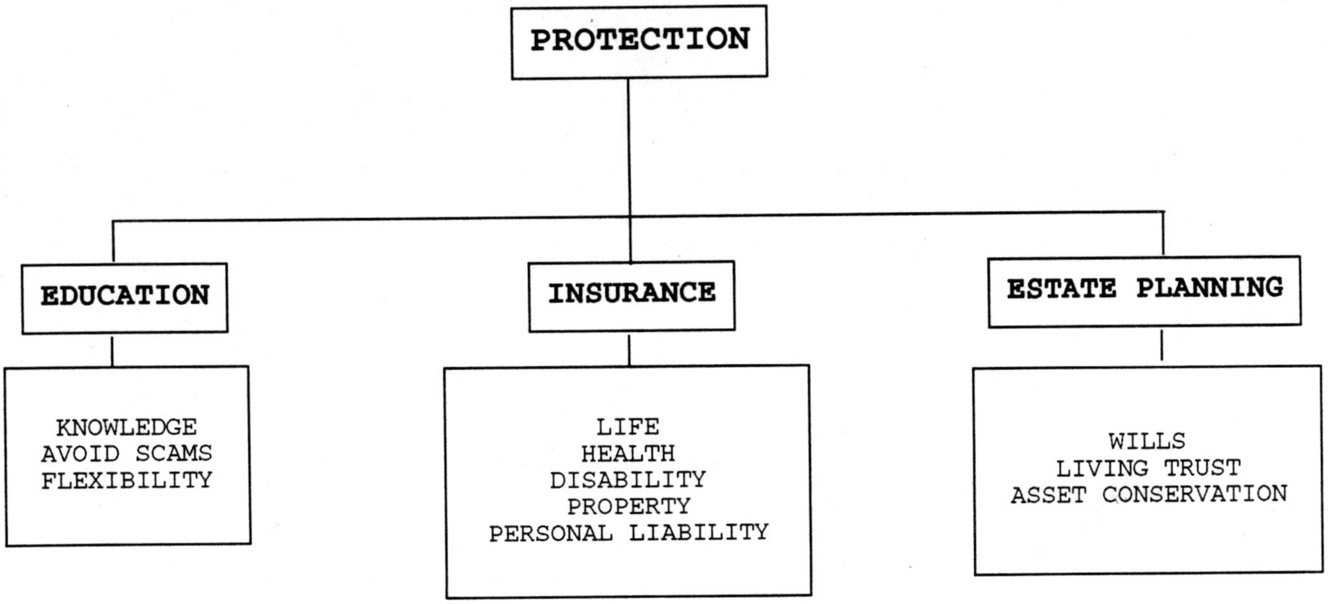

THE TEN COMMANDMENTS OF FINANCIAL SECURITY

1. If you don't understand it, don't buy it. If you are unsure about something, seek advice from someone who you know to be knowledgeable and that you trust.

2. Do not rely solely on the advice of someone who is trying to sell you something.

3. Always ask how much it will cost in total whether it be in the form of commissions, fees, or other charges.

4. Never gamble with your investment dollars. Always be suspicious. There are people who will say and do almost anything to separate you from your money. There are no "get-rich-quick" methods to financial security.

5. Never make fast decisions. Take your time and get all the facts and information you need. And always ask yourself how will this benefit me and what risks are involved. Always do your homework before making a decision.

6. Review your investments periodically to judge how things are doing. Remember it is your money.

7. Diversify your investments to minimize any possible loss.

8. Always ask questions; even if the question is "What else should I know about this?" Remember there are no silly questions, but there are silly answers.

9. Don't ever depend on what we might call the **Babe Ruth Rule** - which says, no matter what I do, all I need is to hit a home run and everything will be okay. Very seldom does that home run ever come in time to save the day.

10. **If it seems to good to be true, it probably is.** If you can't remember anything else about investing, please always remember this one rule. Even though this axiom has been around a long time, some people would like to think that they are the exception to the rule. There are con artists who consistently make their living (and quite frankly they make a very substantial living) by taking these people's money.

Insurance Reference Sources

- A.M. Best Co.
- Standard and Poors
- Moody's Investor Service
- Duff & Phelps Credit Rating
- Weiss Research

TEN STEPS TO A SUCCESSFUL RETIREMENT PLAN

1. Take control of your family's lifestyle expenditures and improve your family budget.

2. Maximize your earning potential.

3. Set up your emergency fund, investment fund, and special purpose fund.

4. Reduce your debts.

5. Determine your investment strategy and start investing for your retirement.

6. Don't be afraid to get professional help from Bank Trust Departments, CPAs, Attorneys, Stock Brokers, Financial Planners, Insurance Agents, or others.

7. Continue to read and review the financial sections of newspapers, financial planning magazines, newsletters, and other publications to keep up to date on current conditions which may affect your plan.

8. Make sure you are adequately insured for life, health, disability, property, and personal liability risks.

9. Begin estate planning by establishing a will.

10. Don't hesitate to review this video seminar and use the materials in this notebook to help you stay on the right track.

USEFUL FORMULAS

RULE OF 72 **T = 72/R**

The **T**ime (in years) needed to **double** a starting investment is determined by dividing the **R**ate of return into **72**. For example: if the interest rate is 6%, than 6 divided into 72 would be 12 years. Therefore the amount of money would double in 12 years.

RULE OF 115 **T = 115/R**

The **T**ime (in years) needed to triple a starting investment is determined by dividing the **R**ate of return into **115**. For example: if the interest rate is 5%, than 5 divided into 115 would be 23 years. Therefore the amount of money would triple in 23 years.

PURCHASE POWER MAINTENANCE FORMULA **R = I/(1-M)**

The **R**ate of return a taxable investment must earn to maintain its purchase power under the effects of inflation is determined by dividing the **I**nflation rate by one minus the **M**arginal tax rate. For example: if inflation is at a rate of 3%, your marginal tax rate is 28%, then 3 divided by (1.00 - .28) .72 is equal to 4.17%. Therefore, a taxable investment must earn 4.17% to maintain its purchasing power under an inflation rate of 3% and your marginal tax rate is 28%.

TAX FREE INVESTMENT COMPARISON FORMULA **T = F/(1-M)**

The return rate necessary for a **T**axable investment to produce the equivalent yield of a tax-free investment is determined by dividing the interest rate of the tax-**F**ree investment by one minus the **M**arginal tax rate. For example: if the interest rate of the tax-free investment is 4% and your marginal tax rate is 28%, then 4 is divided by (1.00 - .28) .72 is equal to 5.56%. Therefore, a taxable investment yielding 5.56% is equal to a tax-free investment of 4%.

BOND CURRENT YIELD **Y = I/P**

Bond Current **Y**ield is determined by dividing the total amount of **I**nterest received on an annual basis by the total **P**rice paid for the bond. For example: if the total interest received for the year was $80.00 and the total purchase price of the bond was $800.00, we would divide $80.00 by $800.00 to determine the current yield to be 10%.

USEFUL FORMULAS
- continued -

RATE OF RETURN **R = CF/P**

Rate of return on an investment is determined similar to that of bond current yield. The total amount of **C**ash **F**low received during the year (whether from interest, dividends, etc.) is divided by the total amount of the original **P**urchase price of the investment. For example: if the total earnings received for the year was $72.00 and the original purchase price of the investment was $900.00, we would divide $72.00 by $900.00 to determine the rate of return to be 8%.

TOTAL RATE OF RETURN **TR = CF ± I(D)/P**

Total **R**ate of return on an investment is determined by taking the total amount of **C**ash **F**low received during the year (whether from interest, dividends, etc.) and either adding the **I**ncrease in value between the original purchase price of the investment and the current value of the investment or subtracting the **D**ecrease in value then dividing this amount by the original **P**urchase price of the investment. For example: if the total earnings received for the year was $72.00 and the current value of the investment is $1,100.00 and the original price of the investment was $900.00, we would add $72.00 to the increase in value ($1,100.00 - $900.00 = $300.00) and divide by $900.00 to determine the total rate of return to be 41.3% ($72.00 + $300.00 = $372.00/$900.00 = 41.3%)

ADVISORY DIRECTORY

Information and recommendations on life insurance companies:

National Insurance Consumer Organization
121 North Payne Street
Alexandria, Virginia 22314

Insurance Quote
(800) 972-1104

Select Quote
(800) 343-1985

Insurance Information
(800) 472-5800

Quotesmith Corporation
(800) 556-9393

Information and recommendations on healthcare policies:

Quotesmith Corporation
(800) 556-9393

GLOSSARY

ACCIDENTAL DEATH BENEFIT. Provides that the death benefit will be paid if death is due to an accident rather than illness.

ACCOUNTING EQUATION. An algebraic expression of financial position: Assets = Liabilities + Equity.

ACCOUNTING TAX RECORDS. A taxpayer's regular books of account and such other records and data as may be necessary to support the income reported and deductions taken on his or her tax return.

ACCUMULATED DEPRECIATION. The total past depreciation on a specific asset.

ACCUMULATION DISTRIBUTION. Resulting amount when current distributions exceed distributable net income for a trust or estate.

ACTUARY. A professional insurance statistician who calculates risk, premiums, defined benefit plans and related matters.

ADJUSTABLE RATE MORTGAGE. The interest rate may be moved up or down by the lender, at specified intervals, such as every six months, or thirty months, or three years.

ADJUSTED GROSS ESTATE (AGE). Gross income less allowable deductions result in AGE.

ADJUSTED GROSS INCOME (AGI). For federal income tax purposes is found at the bottom of page 1 of the form 1040. Gross income less adjustments to gross income equals Adjusted Gross Income (AGI).

ADMINISTRATOR. The person appointed by a court to administer and settle the estate of a person who has died without a will or the estate of a person whose will appoints an executor who cannot serve.

ADVISER. The person or company that a mutual fund employs to manage the fund's investments.

AGGRESSIVE GROWTH FUND. A fund that seeks maximum capital gains. It usually remains fully invested in stocks at all times; it buys small, speculative companies and depressed stocks; and it may employ techniques like selling short and using leverage. Aggressive growth funds tend to be especially volatile.

AICPA. A professional organization of Certified Public Accountants, called the American Institute of Certified Public Accountants.

ALL-WEATHER FUND. A fund that does well in bull and bear markets.

ALPHA. Number that measures how well a fund has performed, considering it's volatility. An alpha above 0 is considered desirable.

ALTERNATE VALUATION DATE. Valuation date six months after the decedent's date of death. For estate tax purposes, the executor may place a value on the estate as of the date of death or on the alternate valuation date, generally choosing the date on which the total value is lower.

ALTERNATIVE MINIMUM TAX. A special tax targeted at high-income people who have benefitted from certain tax deductions to lower their regular income tax.

A.M. BEST & COMPANY. An independent firm that rates annuities, insurance companies, etc.

AMORTIZATION. A method of liquidating (paying off) a debt by making periodic payments of the principal and interest over a fixed period of time; The systematic allocation of the cost of an intangible asset to expense over its useful life.

ANNUAL GIFT TAX EXCLUSION. The amount that may be excluded from the gift tax. Donors may exclude up to $10,000 per year per donee.

ANNUAL PERCENTAGE RATE (APR). The finance charge over a full year expressed as a percentage, reflecting all the costs of the loan.

ANNUAL REPORT. Formal report to stockholder's that includes a financial statement issued yearly by the management of a company.

ANNUITANT. The person who establishes and receives the benefits of an annuity.

ANNUITIZE. The process of converting accumulated savings into periodic payments.

ANNUITY. An investment usually made through an insurance company that grows tax-deferred until withdrawn. It can also be an immediate annuity, which entitles the investor to a specific sum each year for life and/or the lifetime of another under a contractual arrangement with an insurance company.

ANTENUPTIAL AGREEMENT. Usually prepared prior to entering into a second marriage, it sets forth the details of property distribution in case of the death of one of the partners. Also called a premarital agreement.

APPRECIATION. Growth in value of an asset.

APPROVED CHARGE. When a medical insurance claim is submitted, the carrier compares the actual charge

shown on the claim with the customary and prevailing charges for that service or supply. The charge approved by the carrier will be either the customary charge, the prevailing charge, or the actual charge, whichever is lowest. Medicare pays 80 percent of the approved charge, sometimes referred to as the reasonable charge.

ARBITRAGE. Strategy to profit from differences in the price of the same investment that is traded in two or more markets. Also, the buying and selling of an investment in a short period of time for a profit.

ASKED OR OFFERING PRICE. Price at which an investment can be purchased. The amount the purchaser has to pay to buy an investment.

ASSET ALLOCATION. How you invest the money in your investment portfolio among stocks, bonds, real estate, cash equivalents, etc. Diversification by choice.

ASSET ALLOCATION FUND. A fund that either keeps a fixed percentage of its assets in various investment vehicles or varies the percentages, depending on where the fund manager thinks the investment markets are heading.

ASSETS. All money, investments and other property owned by an individual, a family, or a business. It is everything that you own.

ASSIGNMENT. When a doctor or supplier accepts an assignment of the medical insurance payment, he or she agrees that the total charge to you for covered services will be the charge approved by the carrier. The doctor or supplier can charge you only for the part of the deductible you have not met and for the coinsurance, which is the remaining 20 percent of the approved charge.

AT-RISK RULES. Income tax provisions that limit the amount of tax losses an investor can deduct against their other taxable income.

ATTESTATION CLAUSE. A clause at the end of a will stating that all the witnesses were present when the testator signed the will.

ATTORNEY IN FACT. The person or entity named in the power of attorney to act in the place of the person granting the power.

AUTOMATIC REINVESTMENT. A decision to have distributions (interest, dividends and/or capital gains) reinvested in more of the same type of investment instead of actually taking the money as a distribution. See Dollar Cost Averaging example in notebook.

AVERAGE INDEXED MONTHLY EARNINGS (AIME). Social Security benefits are based on indexed earnings, which reflect the impact of inflation and higher earnings levels at present as compared with the 1950s and 1960s, when average earnings ranged from $2,800 to $6,000. For example, if a worker's earnings in 1956 were $3,000, this amount would be adjusted to about $9,000. These adjusted earnings are averaged to obtain a benefit rate that is more in line with today's earnings. This method is used for all people retiring on or after January 1, 1984.

BACK-END LOAD. A charge when you sell shares of certain mutual funds. Also called deferred sales charge.

BALANCED MUTUAL FUND. A fund that invest in both stocks and bonds in approximately an even ratio - commonly 50% in stocks, 50% in bonds.

BALANCE SHEET. An accounting statement that provides information about the assets, liabilities and owners' equity of a company or individual as of a particular date.

BANKRUPTCY. A court proceeding in which an individual or business entity declares that they are unable to pay their debts and seeks the protection of the court and the court's guidance in an effort to remove or reduce those debts.

BASIC VALUE INVESTING. Investment strategy that concentrates on buying seemingly undervalued stocks, based on their price-earnings ratio, price to book value and other indicators.

BASIS. The original cost of the property or asset plus any additional capital expenditures made since the purchase of the property or asset.

BASIS POINT. In bond yields, 0.01%. If a bond's yield goes from 8% to 9%, it has increased by 100 basis points.

BEAR. Person who believes that stock prices in general will drop. Opposite of someone who is called a "Bull" who believes that the stock prices in general will increase.

BEARER BOND. Does not have the owner's name registered on the books of the issuer or on the certificate. Interest and principal, when due, are payable to the holder or bearer of the certificate.

BEAR MARKET. An investment environment in which prices of securities are either falling or expected to fall for a prolonged period. See Bull Market.

BEFORE DEATH OPTION. An insurance option where the policy pays out the death benefit before the policyholder dies in order to pay the nursing home, medical treatment or long-term care. Also called living insurance, living benefit option, living needs benefit, or accelerated death benefit.

BENEFICIARY. Person who is entitled to the benefits from trust property, insurance policy proceeds or who inherits under a will.

BEQUEST. A gift of property under a trust or will. Also called legacy.

BETA COEFFICIENT. Comparison of the volatility of an investment with the Standard & Poor's 500 stock index, which is given a beta of 1. Beta is sometimes equated with riskiness.

BID. Current price at which a buyer is willing to purchase a security. The bid is the net proceeds the seller receives from the sale of an investment after paying the dealer's markup or spread.

BID OR REDEMPTION (SELL) PRICE. Price at which a mutual fund shares can be redeemed or sold back to the fund. The bid price does not take into account any redemption fee or back-end load.

BINDER. A deposit requested by a seller to hold a piece of property for an interested buyer until a set date.

BLUE BOOK. A publication of the National Automobile Dealers Association (NADA) that lists the average price paid for used cars at a specified time.

BLUE CHIP STOCK. A stock in a company known nationally for the quality and wide acceptance of its product or services. Also known for it's ability to earn large profits and to pay dividends regularly.

BLUE-COLLAR WORKER. Anyone whose job requires manual labor and who wears work cloths or other specialized clothing on the job.

BLUE-SKY LAW. Legislation passed by individual states to protect investors. (A judge once said that one worthless stock offering had the value of a patch of blue sky.)

BOND. A debt instrument to repay a loan on a specified date while paying the bondholder a specified amount of interest at regular intervals usually twice a year, whether or not the company issuing the bond is making money. Debt instrument holders must be paid before a company pays any distributions to owners of its stock.

BOND FUND. A fund that invests mainly in corporate, municipal, and U.S. Treasury securities. Such a fund emphasizes income rather than capital gains.

BOND RATING. Method of grading bonds by the issuer's ability to continue paying interest and to repay the bond holder's principal. Standard & Poor's ratings range from AAA (extremely unlikely to default) to D (in default). Moody's ratings are similar.

BOOKKEEPING. Recording of transactions according to a system of accounting.

BOOK VALUE. For an asset, cost less accumulated depreciation or amortization; for each share of common stock, common stockholders' equity divided by the outstanding shares.

BOTTOM UP. Method of investing in which the investor concentrates on buying attractive stocks, whatever the overall trends of the market or the economy.

BROKERAGE FIRM. A business that buys and sells securities to the public for a commission.

BROKER/DEALER. Firms or individuals that buy and sell securities to the public for a commission.

BUDGET. A spending plan designed to help you manage your income efficiently by controlling income and expenses.

BUILD-UP PHASE. The period of time that cash contributions to an annuity are being made.

BULL. Person who believes that stock prices in general will rise. Opposite of someone who is called a "Bear" who believes that the stock prices in general will drop.

BULLION. Gold or silver in bars or ingots, not as coins.

BULL MARKET. An investment environment in which prices of securities are either rising or expected to rise. These markets usually last at least several months, sometimes several years. See Bear Market.

BUSINESS RISK. An unsystematic risk involving the possibility that cash flow is inadequate to sustain a business enterprise.

BUY AND HOLD. Investment strategy that entails buying shares of stock or a mutual fund for the long term and selling them only in special circumstances, such as after a long-term loss.

BUY-SELL AGREEMENT. A tool for transferring the portion of an individual's ownership of a business to designated heirs with the surviving owners retaining control of the business.

CALLABLE. A bond or preferred stock, which may be redeemed by the issuing corporation under specified conditions before maturity.

CALLABLE BOND. A bond that can be paid off by the issuing company before its scheduled maturity.

CALL OPTION. A right to buy a fixed number of shares of stock at a specified price within a limited period of time. The purchaser hopes that the stock's price will go up by an amount sufficient to provide a profit when the option is sold. If the stock price remains the same or goes down, the investment in the call option is lost. (See Put Option.)

CAPITAL. Money or its equivalent in property and securities.

CAPITAL GAIN. The profit received from the sale of an investment asset, such as a stock, bond, mutual fund, or real estate.

CAPITAL LOSS. The loss resulting from the sale or exchange of a capital asset, such as a stock, bond, mutual fund, or real estate.

CAPITAL STOCK. The amount invested by the owners of the business; a general term for common stock.

CASH. Cash or cash equivalents like certificates of deposit or treasury securities.

CASH DIVIDENDS. Distributions to stockholders in cash.

CASH EQUIVALENTS. Money you lend for a short time, as in Money-market fund, Treasury bills, and CDs that come due in a year or less.

CASH FLOW. Cash income from all sources whether earned or from investments, less cash expenses.

CASH FLOW STATEMENT. A financial statement disclosing the cash receipts and cash payments during an accounting period.

CASH REFUND ANNUITY. Pays income to the insured for life, but if the insured dies before the payments equal the amount the insured put into the annuity less specified administrative charges, the balance is paid to the insured's beneficiary or beneficiaries in a lump sum.

CASH SURRENDER VALUE. Amount that an insurance policy owner is entitled to receive from their investment in an insurance policy if coverage is discontinued. Also called cash value.

CASUALTY AND THEFT LOSSES. Losses to your assets because of a sudden, unexpected or unusual event, such as a fire, flood or theft.

CATASTROPHIC MAJOR MEDICAL INSURANCE. Provides compensation for extraordinary medical costs not covered by hospitalization insurance, or by basic or major medical insurance.

CATS. A zero coupon bond issued by the U.S. government, called Certificates of Accrual on Treasury Securities.

CENTRAL LISTING SERVICE. Information on real estate units for sale or rent is made available to all member real estate brokers in a given area. Even though the property may have been listed with one of them, each has the right to sell or rent, splitting the commission with the broker who obtained the listing. Also called Multiple Listing Service.

CERTIFICATE OF ACCRUAL ON TREASURY SECURITIES (CATS). Securities that represent ownership of interest or principal payments on U.S. Treasury notes or bonds, which in turn are direct obligations of the U.S. government. CATS are taxable zero coupon securities that are extremely liquid.

CERTIFICATE OF DEPOSIT (CD). A type of savings deposit available to anyone who deposits a specified sum of money for a set period of time. Currently each bank can set its own rates, terms, and minimum deposits. A CD usually carries a penalty for early withdrawal before the maturity date stated on the certificate.

CERTIFIED FINANCIAL PLANNER. Designation given by the College for Financial Planning to individuals who successfully complete a five-course curriculum.

CERTIFIED PUBLIC ACCOUNTANT. A professional who has successfully passed a five part exam and is licensed and regulated by state boards in accounting.

CHARITABLE TRUST. Trust originated in an effort to make one or more gifts to a charitable organization.

CLASSIFIED HELP WANTED ADS. Listings of job opportunities published in newspapers and magazines.

CHATTEL MORTGAGE. The buyer acquires title or ownership to the purchased property but pledges it as security for the balance due of a mortgage note. Failure to meet the payments gives the lender, usually a financial institution or finance company, the right to foreclose the loan, repossess the item, and sue for the remaining balance plus court costs.

CLIFF VESTING. Qualifying for the benefits of a pension plan all at once, after a specific time has laps (generally 5 years), but not being qualified for any benefits before that time.

CLONE FUND. A fund that imitates another fund, which may have become excessively large and is closed to new investors.

CLOSED FUND. A fund that has stopped issuing new shares. Funds close either because they are so large that the managers cannot find enough good investments, or because the manager prefers investing only in small companies, and cannot cope with large amounts of money.

CLOSED-END MUTUAL FUND. A mutual fund whose shares are bought and sold on an exchange or over-the-counter, by investors trading among themselves. A closed-end fund issued only a limited number of shares. See Open-End Investment Company.

CLOSING COSTS. Costs resulting from the financing and transfer of property ownership in a real estate sale.

COBRA RIGHTS. Federal statute guaranteeing continuation of medical coverage of an employer sponsored group insurance policy for a certain number of months where the premiums are paid for by the person insured, not the employer.

CODICIL. An amendment to a will that must be signed and witnessed with the same formality as a will.

CO-EXECUTOR. An additional executor, perhaps your spouse, to work with the executor.

COINSURANCE. The percentage of an expense covered by a policy that you are required to pay. For example, you pay 20 percent of the approved charge; the insurer pays 80 percent.

COLA (COST OF LIVING ADJUSTMENT). Annual increase in Social Security benefits, helping to protect recipients against inflation.

COLLATERALIZED MORTGAGE OBLIGATION. A debt security that is secured by high-quality mortgage-backed securities.

COLLECTIBLE. An item purchased for its value with the hopes that the value will increase and thus yield a profit when it is ultimately sold. Items include jewelry, diamonds, rare books, paintings, other art works, stamps, antiques, oriental rugs, and so forth.

COLLISION COVERAGE. First party auto insurance that pays for damage to your auto from collisions.

COMMERCIAL PAPER. Short-term promises to pay issued by corporations, usually 60 days or less.

COMMISSION. A percentage of sales paid to a salesman or agent; For a mutual fund, the percentage of the sales price paid to the mutual fund to cover the fund's cost of selling the product and commissions that it pays its agents or brokers.

COMMODITY. Items that can be owned.

COMMODITY FUTURE. Agreement to purchase or sell a specific amount of commodity at a particular price on a stipulated future date.

COMMON STOCK. Securities that represent an ownership interest in a corporation and the right to share in profits, known as dividends, after the company pays its expenses and prior claims. Owners of common stock have the potential of earning not only dividends but also capital appreciation.

COMMON STOCK MUTUAL FUND. Money is invested primarily in common stocks. This is the most popular form of mutual fund.

COMMUNITY PROPERTY. In eight states (Arizona, California, Idaho, Louisiana, Nevada, New Mexico, Texas, and Washington), the laws provide that property acquired after marriage is considered to be equally owned, 50 percent each, no matter who contributes the money to pay for the property.

COMPOUNDING. The process of earning interest on the interest already earned on an investment. When interest is left to accumulate, compound interest is earned. The sooner the periodic payments of interest the faster the investment compounds or grows.

COMPREHENSIVE COVERAGE. First party auto insurance that pays for damage to your auto from theft, vandalism or damage from falling objects.

COMPREHENSIVE MAJOR MEDICAL INSURANCE. Provides coverage for the same types of services that are covered under basic health insurance plans; that is, hospitalization, medical, and surgical, picking up where basic protection ends. Some policies provide for first-dollar coverage of some health care services, and others may have high deductibles.

COMPRESSED WORK WEEK. A rearrangement of time so that more hours are worked some days with no hours on other days. For example, five 8-hour days can be compressed into four 10-hour days.

CONCURRENT OWNERSHIP. Ownership and control of property by more than one person at the same time.

CONDITIONAL GIFT. A gift that is received but must be returned if a certain event takes place.

CONDITIONAL SALES AGREEMENT. A type of contract in which the buyer of an item agrees to pay a specified amount of money per month for a given number of months. Ownership or title remains with the seller until the final installment has been paid by the buyer. Failure to meet the payments gives the seller the right to repossess the item. Also called installment agreement.

CONDOMINIUM. A legal plan of ownership of property whereby the purchaser of a condominium owns the space he or she occupies and shares ownership of common elements with other condominium owners.

CONSERVATOR. A court-appointed administrator who is designated to look after the financial affairs of an individual who is still living and who is incapable of handling such matters as picking up mail, handling checks and bank transactions, and paying bills.

CONSIDERATION. Something of value that makes a contract legally binding, usually some value agreed upon by the individuals entering the agreement.

CONSUMER CREDIT PROTECTION ACT. A Federal act that includes the Fair Credit Billing, Equal Credit Opportunity, Fair Credit Reporting, Consumer Leasing Acts, and the Truth in Lending Act.

CONSUMER PRICE INDEX (CPI). An index, prepared by the U.S. Department of Labor, Bureau of Labor Statistics, reflecting monthly changes in the relative cost of a specific market basket of goods and services as measured against a base year.

CONTENTS INSURANCE. Coverage on the contents of a home including furnishings, typically part of basic homeowner's coverage.

CONTINGENT BENEFICIARY. Party who receives the death benefit if the primary beneficiary predeceases the insured. Also called second in line.

CONTINGENT LIABILITIES. A potential liability whose outcome depends upon some future event.

CONTINGENT REMAINDER. Interest in an estate that does not come into enjoyment and possession unless a certain condition or contingency occurs; or, an interest that may terminate upon the occurrence (or non-occurrence) of an event in the future.

CONTRACT. A legally binding agreement between two or more parties in which, for a consideration, one or more of the parties agrees to do or not to do a certain thing.

CONTRARIAN INVESTING. Buying securities when other investors are pessimistic, selling securities when other investors are optimistic. Sometimes called going opposite of the crowd.

CONTRIBUTORY PENSION PLAN. Both the employer and the employee share the cost of the contribution in some prescribed proportion.

CONVENTIONAL MORTGAGE. A home loan with fixed monthly payments covering interest and amortization for the life of the loan, and usually not insured by the Federal Housing Administration or guaranteed by the Veterans Administration. Also called a fixed rate mortgage.

CONVERSION. Transformation of an existing insurance policy into another type of policy.

CONVERSION PRIVILEGE. Right of a shareholder to switch from one fund in a family of funds to another fund in that family.

CONVERTIBLE. A bond or preferred stock that may be exchanged by the owner for common stock or another security, usually of the same company, in accordance with the terms of the issue.

CONVERTIBLE SECURITY. A bond or share of preferred stock that can be exchanged into a specified amount of common stock at a specified price under certain circumstances.

COOPERATIVE. A legal plan of ownership of property in which the purchaser buys shares in a corporation that owns the land and the entire structure or complex. The purchaser cannot get a mortgage but may get a loan to purchase the shares. If the occupant wishes to sell his or her shares, permission must be obtained from the board of directors of the cooperative.

COORDINATION OF BENEFITS. Limitation of benefits when an individual is covered by two or more insurance policies.

CO-PAYMENT. Amount that insured must pay toward a claim; normally phased out at a particular dollar level. Also called deductible.

CORPORATE BOND. Long-term IOU of a corporation secured by specific assets or a promise to pay; generally issued in units of $1,000.

CORPORATION. A legal entity which, within the scope of its charter issued by a state, is treated as a natural person. It may make contracts; own, buy, and sell property; incur debts; sue and be sued in a court of law. The corporation enjoys perpetual life, and the stockholders enjoy limited liability. A form of business organization recognized as a separate entity distinct from its owners.

CORPUS. The Latin term for "body". In the legal sense, corpus refers to the principal of an estate or a bequest. Every trust must have a corpus.

COSIGNER. Someone who agrees to accept responsibility for a loan if the original borrower defaults.

COST BASIS. The original price that you paid plus any additional improvements or investments to an asset.

COST-OF-LIVING ADJUSTMENTS (COLA). An annual increase in Social Security benefits designed to protect retirement income against inflation. The Social Security Amendments of 1983 established January as the month for the annual COLA increase.

COUPON BOND. Postdated interest coupons are attached to the bond, and are clipped as they become due. The coupon or coupons are presented at a bank for deposit or exchanged for cash. The bank collects from the issuing corporation or government.

COUPON RATE. Stated rate of interest that an issuer will pay its bondholders expressed as an annual

percentage of face value.

CPI (Consumer Price Index). An index, prepared by the U.S. Department of Labor, Bureau of Labor Statistics, reflecting monthly changes in the relative cost of a specific market basket of goods and services as measured against a base year.

CREDIT. Loans to individuals, businesses, or governments.

CREDIT CARD. A type of credit activated by the presentation of a plastic card allowing the cardholder to purchase items from any business that accepts the card for payment.

CREDIT LIFE INSURANCE. Life insurance covering the repayment of a loan should the borrower die.

CREDIT SCORING. An objective method of evaluating whether an individual is a good credit risk.

CREDIT UNION. A depository financial institution formed as a cooperative by individuals who are associated in some way - either employment or profession.

CRUMMEY POWERS. The right to annually withdraw certain amounts from a trust without adverse tax consequences. The name comes from the court case which brought about the law.

CUMULATIVE PREFERRED STOCK. A security which has a provision that if one or more dividends are omitted, the omitted dividends must be paid before dividends may be paid on the company's common stock.

CURRENCY TRANSACTION REPORTS (CTRs). Banks are required to file with the Treasury Department a report for cash transactions exceeding $10,000.

CURRENT ASSETS. Assets that can be readily converted into cash within a short period of time.

CURRENT LIABILITIES. Debts or portions of debts payable within one year.

CURRENT RATIO. Current assets divided by current liabilities.

CURRENT YIELD. Annual earnings (interest or dividends) paid to investors as a percentage of the current price.

CUSTODIAL CARE. Primarily for the purpose of meeting personal needs, such as helping in walking, getting in and out of bed, bathing, dressing, eating, taking medicine, and other services which can be provided by persons without professional skills or training. Medicare does not cover custodial care.

CUSTODIAN. A person or entity acting as representative of a minor or an incompetent person.

CUSTOMARY CHARGE. Generally the fee most frequently charged by doctors and suppliers for specific services and supplies furnished to patients in the previous calendar year.

CYCLICAL STOCK. Stock that tends to rise quickly when the economy turns up and to fall quickly when the economy turns down. These stocks are directly affected by economic changes such as housing, automobiles, and paper products.

DATE OF GIFT. Date the donor's control over the property ceases and is transferred to another.

DATE OF RECORD. The date on which all investors in a security or fund become entitled to receive declared interest or dividends.

DEATH CERTIFICATE. A document, signed by a doctor, medical examiner or coroner, giving pertinent information about a deceased person, such as name, age, date, time, place, and cause of death.

DEATH TAXES. Those taxes imposed on the property that is transferred to another upon the death of an individual. Death taxes include the Federal estate tax and state inheritance and estate taxes.

DEBENTURE BOND. Backed by the general credit of the issuer and not by any specified piece of property.

DEBT/EQUITY RATIO. Total liabilities divided by total owners' or stockholders' equity.

DEBT RATIO. Total liabilities divided by the sum of liabilities and stockholders' equity.

DECEDENT. A legal term referring to a person who has died.

DECREASING TERM INSURANCE. Term insurance with a level premium but a decreasing death benefit.

DEDUCTIBLE. The annual maximum amount you must pay on claims before the insurance carrier begins to calculate benefit allowances due you. Also called co-payment.

DEDUCTIONS. Amounts you can subtract from your adjusted gross income, such as for charitable contributions, real estate taxes, state income taxes and employee business expenses.

DEED. A written instrument that conveys title to real property.

DEFENSIVE STOCK. Stock which tend to do well during economically rough times.

DEFERRED ANNUITY. Begins to pay out after several years as opposed to an immediate annuity that starts paying out immediately.

DEFERRED SALES CHARGE. The sales charge you pay when you sell the shares of a mutual fund. Usually expressed in a percentage of the original investment and decreases the longer that you hold the investment.

DEFICIT. The amount by which expenditures exceed income.

DEFINED BENEFIT PLAN. A pension plan in which your monthly retirement allowance is tied to both years of credited service and salary. The employee usually can contribute to the plan, but the employer is responsible for contributing enough into the pension fund to buy an annuity that will provide the defined monthly benefit.

DEFINED CONTRIBUTION PLAN. A retirement plan where the employer makes contributions determined by a formula most often expressed as a percentage of earnings. Some plans require a fixed contribution and other plans provide for discretionary contributions by the employer.

DEFLATION. A decrease in the general level of prices for goods and services. Opposite of inflation.

DELAYED RETIREMENT CREDIT (DRC). The percentage of additional cash benefits awarded for each year of additional work after normal retirement age during which an eligible individual does not draw benefits from the Social Security Administration.

DEPENDENT. A qualified person for whom you provide over half the support and are therefore entitled to a exemption allowance on your personal individual income tax return. Check the instruction of your Income Tax Booklet for who qualifies for being claimed as a dependent.

DEPLETION. The allocation of the cost of natural resources to expense as they are used or consumed.

DEPRECIATION. A yearly deduction you can take on business and investment assets that presumably lose value as they grow older, even though in actuality they might be increasing in value. An example of an asset that can be depreciated but really is going up in value would be a building.

DISABILITY. Applies when you are so severely physically or mentally disabled that you are unable to do any substantial gainful work, and when the condition is expected to last at least 12 months or is expected to result in death. You and your dependents are eligible for benefits from the Social Security Administration at any age if you become disabled.

DISABILITY BENEFITS. Some insurance plans provide benefits if an employee is unable to work because of illness or disability. Plans vary in their definitions of "disability" as well as age and service requirements which determine eligibility for these benefits.

DISABILITY INCOME INSURANCE. Provides a percentage of your regular income when you are unable to work for an extended period of time because of illness or injury. This is the most overlooked form of insurance.

DISABILITY INSURANCE. A Social Security benefit which protects you, your spouse, and your children during your working years by providing benefits if you are unable to work for an extended period of time because of an illness or other disability. The amount of your disability benefit is your primary insurance amount at the time you become disabled. There is no reduction in your primary insurance amount if you start receiving the benefit before age 65.

DISCLAIMER. Allows a person to postpone decisions that are based upon asset values and estate composition until such values are fixed at death.

DISCOUNT. Investment that sells for less than its face value. A discount bond trades for less than what the issuer will pay when the bond comes due.

DISCOUNT RATE. Rate of interest charged by the Federal Reserve to it's member banks.

DISTRIBUTIONS. The transfer of assets according to the percent of ownership or to the terms of a will, or trust.

DISTRIBUTOR. The entity that holds the assets to be distributed.

DIVERSIFICATION. The allocation of your investment fund over a variety of different investments to reduce risk and realize a reasonable return.

DIVERSIFIED INVESTMENT COMPANY. Company whose investments are limited to no more than 5% in a single issue, and no more than 10% of the issuer's outstanding securities; at least 75% of its assets must be in varied securities.

DIVIDENDS. The payment to the holder of common stock or preferred stock by a corporation. On common stock, the dividend varies with the earnings of the company and may be omitted if business is bad. On preferred stock, the dividend is usually a fixed amount.

DIVIDENDS FROM INSURANCE COMPANY. Are not dividends at all but really the return of part of your insurance premiums by a mutual insurance company because you were actually over charged.

DIVIDEND YIELD PERCENTAGE. The annual cash dividend per share divided by the current market price of the stock.

DOLLAR-COST AVERAGING. Investing the same amount of money at regular intervals, so that when securities are low-priced you buy more shares. A method of diversifying the prices at which you buy securities.

DOMICILE. The state in which a person has a permanent (legal) residence.

DONEE. Person receiving a gift from the donor of the gift.

DONOR. Person making or giving a gift to the donee.

DOUBLE INDEMNITY CLAUSE. Provides that the death benefit will be doubled or even tripled if death is due to an accident rather than illness.

DOWER. Statutory provision in a common-law state that directs a certain portion of the estate (often 1/3) to the surviving wife. The term curtesy is used if the surviving spouse is the husband.

DOW JONES INDUSTRIAL AVERAGE. It consists of 30 blue-ship stocks and is considered a model for the stock market as a whole.

DOWN PAYMENT. The cash a buyer puts toward a purchase, with the remainder of the purchase cost to be paid when the buyer actually receives the items purchased.

DURABLE POWER OF ATTORNEY. A power of attorney that remains in effect even when the giver of the power becomes incompetent.

EARNED INCOME. Money you receive from your job or business, contrasted with unearned income, which is derived from other sources, such as investments.

EARNINGS LIMITATION FOR EMPLOYEES (RETIREMENT TEST). If you continue to work after your Social Security benefits start, you are subject to the earnings limitation, under which your benefits are reduced by $1 for every $2 you earn over the earnings limitation. No earnings limitation applies when you reach the age of 70.

EARNINGS PER SHARE. Total amount of net income of a corporation divided by the total number of shares of common stock.

EFFICIENT MARKET. Theory that all securities are properly priced, and investors will do better than average only in proportion to the extra risks they take.

ELDER-LAW. A legal specialty devoted to planning for long-term health care and the rights of incompetent elderly people.

ELECTIVE SHARE. A state statutory right of a surviving spouse to get a percentage of the decedent spouse's estate, usually one-third, regardless of how much was specified in a will or trust.

ELIMINATION PERIOD. The first days of confinement in a hospital or other health care facility that are not covered by a health insurance policy.

EMERGENCY FUND. An individual's cash reserve that will serve as a cushion in case of an unexpected emergency in an amount equal to the cost of living for five or six months, depending on individual needs.

EMPLOYEE STOCK OWNERSHIP PLAN (ESOP). Form of company-sponsored savings plan where the employees are buying the company's stock.

EMPLOYMENT AGENCY. An organization that helps people find jobs. The services of a public agency are free; private agencies charge a fee.

ENDOWMENT INSURANCE POLICY. A cash value life insurance policy that assesses premiums over a specified period of time. At the end of that time, the cash value equals the face value and is redeemed.

EQUITIES. Stocks, real estate, other assets that an investor owns, as opposed to bonds, where an investor lends money.

EQUITY. The net investment in a business enterprise or in a home that represents ownership.

EQUITY REIT. A real estate investment trust that concentrates on buying shares of real estate companies.

ESCHEAT. The forfeiture of property to the state where a decedent resided at the time of death.

ESCROW. The deposit of money and documents in the custody of a neutral third party until the terms and conditions of an agreement or contract are fulfilled.

ESCROW ACCOUNT. A segregated trust account used to hold funds pending the closing of a transaction.

ESTATE. A body of assets that encompasses all of an individual's real and personal property at the time of their death.

ESTATE PLANNING. The process of analyzing your assets and liabilities, managing and conserving them effectively during your lifetime, and disposing of them at your death through a will or living trust

so as to best serve the needs of your beneficiaries and reduce your estates death and transfer taxes.

ESTATE TAX. Tax imposed on the fair market value of all assets, held by a person at death, less liabilities and the exclusion of $600,000 prior to its distribution.

ESTIMATED TAXES. Income taxes you must pay in advance, four times a year, when the taxes withheld from your wages are not equal to at least 90 percent of the total tax you expect to owe.

EVENT RISK. The danger that a asset will lose value because of special situations, such as the issuer of a bond being subject to a leveraged buy-out and acquiring a great deal of new debt.

EXCHANGE PRIVILEGE. The right of a shareholder to switch from one fund in a family to another fund in the same family of mutual funds.

EXCLUSION (INSURANCE). An expense or condition that the policy does not cover and which it will not pay.

EXCLUSIVE LISTING. A written agreement that gives one real estate broker the right to sell a property for a specified period of time. This does not restrict the right of the owner to sell the property on his or her own but the owner will still have to pay a commission to the broker. Also called exclusive right to sell listing.

EX DISTRIBUTION. The date on which distributions from a mutual fund are deducted from its assets.

EX DIVIDEND. The time between the announcement of a dividend and the actual payment. During this time, new investors are not entitled to the dividend.

EXECUTOR (EXECUTRIX, IF A WOMAN). A person nominated by the individual who writes a will to carry out the directions and requests in the will.

EXEMPTIONS. Subtractions from your taxable income for you, your spouse and certain dependents.

EXIT FEES. Back end fees paid when selling shares of mutual funds. These fees are reduced the longer you hold onto the shares.

EXPENDITURES. Costs incurred and cash outlay.

EXPENSE. Dollar amount of the costs incurred in producing revenues.

EXPENSE RATIO. Measurement of a mutual fund's efficiency in keeping costs down. Annual expenses are divided by average net assets, to factor in economies of scale. Still, large funds usually have lower expense ratio than small ones.

EXTRAORDINARY ITEM. Gains or losses that are unusual in nature and infrequent in occurrence.

FACE VALUE. The stated value of an investment when it comes due, or the stated coverage of a life-insurance policy that will be paid in the event of death.

FAIR MARKET VALUE. Price at which an item would be sold to a willing buyer.

FAIR-WEATHER FUND. A fund that excels in bull markets but gives a mediocre or poor performance in bear markets.

FAMILY. A group of mutual funds under one umbrella, typically consisting of stock fund, a bond fund and a money-market fund.

FANNIE MAES. The nickname for bonds issued by the Federal National Mortgage Association (FNMA), a private corporation created by Congress, to serve as a secondary mortgage market. Fannie Mae bonds may be purchased through a bond broker or by buying into a mutual fund that specializes in these securities.

FEDERAL FUNDS RATE. Interest paid by member banks when borrowing from the Federal Reserve Bank system.

FEDERAL GIFT TAX. Progressive tax levied upon the transfer of gifts from one person to another person.

FEDERAL HOUSING ADMINISTRATION. A U.S. government agency that insures mortgages of qualified buyers against loss due to default, thus encouraging lenders to make mortgage loans on favorable terms.

FEDERAL INSURANCE CONTRIBUTIONS ACT (FICA). This is the Federal law that sets the tax rate and the maximum taxable amount for social security contributions. To increase Social Security taxes, Congress merely amends this law.

FEDERAL RESERVE SYSTEM. Central bank of the United States, which formulates monetary policy and controls the money supply.

FICA. Social Security Tax.

FIDUCIARY. The individual or institution to whom you grant specific rights, duties, and powers to act for you or in your behalf, such as, to carry out the provisions stipulated in your will or for the custody of management of property. An example would be a bank trust department.

FINANCE CHARGE. The total dollar amount you must pay when you borrow a specified amount of money. It includes interest cost, service charges, insurance premiums, and possibly appraisal fees.

FINANCIAL INDEPENDENCE. The ability to enjoy your usual standard of living with income from one or more income sources other than income from your personal services, work or time.

FINANCIAL LEVERAGE. The accelerative effect of debt on financial returns when buying securities or other assets with borrowed money.

FINANCIAL PLANNERS. Advisers of financial affairs.

FINANCIAL PLANNING. Consists of analyzing your net worth (assets minus liabilities), setting financial goals for the future, and then deciding what you must do to achieve those goals.

FINANCIAL RATIOS. Indicators of a company's financial performance and position.

FINANCIAL RISK. Unsystematic risk involving the possibility that cash flow is insufficient to service debt used to finance the business.

FINANCIAL STATEMENTS. The financial reports showing the financial position and results of operations.

FIRST MORTGAGE BONDS. Bonds secured by specific assets.

FIXED DOLLAR ANNUITY. Pays a fixed monthly amount that remains unchanged over the years because the funds in the annuity account are invested in a portfolio of bonds that pay a set amount of interest.

FIXED EXPENSES. Expenses that remain unchanged regardless of changes in output. An example would be rent.

FIXED-INCOME FUNDS. A fund that invests mainly in bonds and preferred stock.

FIXED-INCOME INVESTMENTS. Financial instruments that promise you regular (fixed) payments during their term.

FIXED PREMIUM ANNUITY. An annuity purchased by making a fixed payment each month or each year.

FIXED-RATE ANNUITY. Guarantees a certain rate of return for a specific period of time.

FLEXIBLE LOCATION. A work arrangement under which part of the time is spent working at home while the rest is spent working on the company's premises.

FLEXITIME. A work schedule in which time in and time out are arranged to satisfy special needs of an employee.

FLOATER POLICY. Insurance to protect from damage or theft of jewelry and any other valuable possessions. Added separately to a homeowner's insurance policy.

FLOOD INSURANCE. Federal insurance available in counties susceptible to frequent flood damage.

FORECLOSURE. A procedure by which property pledged as security for a loan is sold or otherwise used to pay the defaulting borrower's debt.

FORMULA INVESTING. Investing according to mechanical techniques, such as dollar-cost averaging.

FORWARD AVERAGING. A method of reducing the tax on assets taken out of certain retirement plans. The money is not taxed at the regular income tax rates but as if it had been withdrawn for five or ten years.

FOUL-WEATHER FUND. A fund that excels in bear markets, one explanation being that the fund invests in securities that are already undervalued.

401(k) PLAN. Is a tax-deferred retirement vehicle offered by an employer for it's employees; also called a salary-reduction plan. Any money that the employee contributes, up to a set limit, to the plan is not taxed for federal income tax purposes and the earnings of the plan accumulate tax deferred.

403(b) PLAN. Is a tax-deferred retirement vehicle offered by an employer for it's employees. Any money that the employee contributes, up to a set limit, to the plan is not income in the year earned and the earning of the plan accumulate tax-deferred.

FRANCHISE. Right or business privilege conferred by law to operate a business using the name and goodwill of another.

FRAUD (TAX). Willful intent by a taxpayer to evade the assessment of a tax.

FREE MARITAL TRANSFER. A deduction from the gross estate for any assets that are transferred to the surviving spouse.

FRONT-END LOAD. A sales commission investors pay at the time they buy shares of a mutual fund. Usually expressed in a percentage of the amount invested.

FUTURES CONTRACT. A contact to buy or sell a given commodity on a future date for a specified price. The market that handles futures contracts, known as the futures market, trades in agricultural products such as wheat, soybeans, pork bellies; metals; and also financial instruments. Businesses utilize futures as a hedge against price changes. Speculators buy and sell futures to profit from price changes.

GENERAL MORTGAGE BOND. Secured by a blanket mortgage on a company's property. Some mortgage bonds are secured by a specific piece of property, such as land, buildings, or machinery.

GENERAL OBLIGATION BOND. A municipal bond whose payment of interest and repayment of principal are backed by the full faith and credit of the issuing government.

GENERAL POWER OF APPOINTMENT. One under which holders have the right to dispose of the property in favor of (1) themselves, (2) their heirs (3) their creditors or (4) the creditors of their estate.

GIFT. A voluntary transfer of property from one person to another without consideration or compensation. Gifts can be given while a person is still living or they can be given after a person's death through a charitable foundation or trust.

GIFT TAX. A tax levied upon the value of a gift after certain specified exemptions. Under Federal law, an individual may give away to one person a maximum of $10,000 each per year. A couple, giving a joint gift, can give a total of $20,000 to each individual per year, which is tax-free to both donor and recipient. Amounts above these are subject to a gift tax. The receiver of the gift does not have to pay income tax on the amount of the gift.

GINNIE MAES (GNMA). The nickname for bonds issued by the Government National Mortgage Association (GNMA), a subsidiary organization of the U.S. Department of Housing and Urban Development, which guarantees funds invested in the mortgage market by institutional investors, such as pension funds. Ginnie Mae bonds may be purchased through a bond broker or by buying into a mutual fund that specializes in these securities.

GLOBAL FUND. A fund that invest in both U.S. and foreign securities.

GNMA FUND. A fund that invests in mortgage securities issued by the Government National Mortgage Association. See Ginnie Maes.

GRADED VESTING. Qualifying for the benefits of a pension plan a portion at a time. Such as 20% after 3 years of employment, 40% after 4 years, 60% after 5 years, 80% after 6 years and 100% after 7 years.

GRADUATED PAYMENT MORTGAGE. A financial arrangement in which the interest rate remains constant but monthly payments start at a low level, rising later to cover the full cost of interest and amortization of the principal.

GRANTOR TRUST. A trust under which the grantor is also the beneficiary of income.

GROSS ESTATE. The value of all of the property counted in the estate of a decedent, wholly or partially owned by the individual at the time of death, before debts and administrative and funeral expenses have been deducted.

GROSS INCOME. Your taxable income from all sources before adjustments to income and deductions for itemized deductions and exemptions.

GROSS NATIONAL PRODUCT (GNP). Measurement of economic activity by computing the total market value of all goods and services produced in a given period.

GROUP TERM INSURANCE. Insurance offered on an open-enrollment basis to all members of a group, such as employees or members of an organization.

GROWTH FUND. A mutual fund that invests in small companies that have the potential to grow in value.

GROWTH STOCK. Stocks that have the ability to grow in value over a period of time.

GUARANTEED INSURABILITY CLAUSE. Allows the insured to continue or increase the amount of insurance coverage without taking a medical exam.

GUARDIAN. A person who has the responsibility to care for a minor or an incompetent adult or to control the property of such an individual or both.

HARD ASSETS. Gold, silver, other precious metals, real estate, antiques and collectibles, and so forth. Financial assets, like stocks and bonds, are "soft" assets.

HEAD OF HOUSEHOLD. An unmarried taxpayer who maintains a residence that's the main home for a dependent for over half the year.

HEALTH MAINTENANCE ORGANIZATION (HMO). Any organized system of health care that provides a full range of health maintenance and treatment services to an enrolled population in return for a fixed sum of money agreed upon and paid in advance. Certain HMOs are eligible for Medicare reimbursement. Such eligible organizations provide (1) physicians services; (2) inpatient hospital services; (3) laboratory, X-ray, emergency, and preventive services, and (4) out-of area coverage.

HEDGE FUND. A fund that not only invests in securities, but may also sell short or write options,

in order to protect itself from losses.

HEIRS. Those who inherit property.

HIGH RISK. Speculative investing containing elements of risk whereby you could lose part or all of your investment. In exchange for this greater risk, you expect a greater potential of higher yields.

HISTORICAL COST. The original cost of an asset.

HOLOGRAPHIC WILL. A will that is handwritten in one's own handwriting, dated and signed. The requirements of witnesses to such a will varies from state to state. Holographic wills are recognized in only about half the states.

HOME EQUITY LOAN. A loan based on the equity of your home, generally for up to 80% of the value of your home less any other mortgages or equity loans.

HOME OWNERS INSURANCE. Policies that insure your home. There are 6 basic types of policies called HO policies.

HOME WARRANTIES. Given by builders, sellers, and real estate brokers to protect home buyers from defects in a home as specified in the contract.

HOSPITAL INSURANCE PROGRAM (HI Program). One of the two separate programs in the Social Security structure. The other is the Old-Age, Survivors, and Disability Insurance program. Each program sets an individual tax. The two taxes are added together and collected as one amount whether you are an employee or self-employed. The Hospital Insurance program pays for hospitalization, which is Part A of medicare. When you become eligible for this benefit, you no longer pay the tax unless you are still working.

HYBRID FUND. A mutual fund that combines the goals of two or more basic mutual funds. Such as a growth and income fund.

"I LOVE YOU" WILL. A will tailored to married couples with small estates in which all assets are left to the surviving spouse.

IMMEDIATE PAY ANNUITY. An annuity that begins to pay out immediately.

INCOME BONDS. Bonds on which interest is payable only if the corporation operates at a profit.

INCOME IN RESPECT OF DECEDENT. Income earned by a decedent prior to his or her death but not yet received.

INCOME MUTUAL FUND. A mutual fund that stresses current income rather than growth of capital. The fund seeks to return a higher level of dividends than other types by investing in high-yielding common stocks, preferred stocks, and bonds.

INCOME PROTECTION INSURANCE. Auto insurance which replaces your wages should you be injured in an auto accident.

INCOME STATEMENT. Financial statement that shows a firm's revenues and expenses over a period of time.

INCOMPETENT. One who is legally unable to handle one's own affairs, usually caused by a physical or mental disability.

INCOMPLETE GIFTS. Gift that does not achieve the objective of removing property from the gross estate of the donor. Includes gifts in contemplation of death, transfers with a retained life interest, transfers taking effect at death and revocable transfers.

INCONTESTABILITY CLAUSE. Prohibits an insurer from challenging the validity of a policy during the entire lifetime of the insured after it has been enforced for a specific time.

INDEMNITY. Protection from loss; an insured will be make whole.

INDEPENDENT AGENT. Agent who sells insurance for two or more companies.

INDEX. A model of an investment market - stocks, bonds, utilities, health-care stocks and so-forth.

INDEXING. The current method for figuring Social Security retirement benefits. Actual earnings for past years are adjusted or indexed to account for changes in average wages since the year the earnings were received. These adjusted earnings are averaged together and the benefit rate is calculated from this average.

INDEX MUTUAL FUNDS. Mutual funds with a portfolio that matches the performance of a broad-based index such as Standard & Poor's 500-Stock Index or the Shearson-Lehman Bond Index.

INDIVIDUAL PROPRIETORSHIP. A form of business organization in which one individual owns and manages, assumes all the risks of, and derives all the profits from, an enterprise.

INDIVIDUAL RETIREMENT ARRANGEMENT (IRA). A personal retirement fund that can be established by an individual with earned income by making contributions up to $2,000 per year. Contributions may or may not be deductible.

INDIVIDUAL RETIREMENT ARRANGEMENT ROLLOVER. A lump-sum payout of your earned retirement benefits from an employer can be rolled over into an Individual Retirement Arrangement tax-free if done within 60 days. This is referred to as an IRA rollover. Be careful of the 20% withholding rules. It is better to make a trustee to trustee transfer to avoid the 20% withholding.

INFLATION. An increase in the general level of prices for goods and services.

INHERITANCE TAX. The state tax imposed on each of the heirs to an estate. The tax rates vary from state to state, and often differ according to the relationship of the heir to the decedent.

INITIAL PUBLIC OFFERING. Corporation's original offering of stock to the public.

INSTALLMENT REFUND ANNUITY. Pays income to the insured for life, but if the insured dies before the payment equals the amount the insured put into the annuity less specified administrative charges, the balance is paid to the insured's beneficiary or beneficiaries in regular payments until they reach that amount.

INSTITUTIONAL INVESTOR. Pension fund, bank, mutual fund, or other huge investor.

INSURABLE INTEREST. Financial interest in property or another person's life; prerequisite to insurability.

INSURANCE BROKER. Typically employs a number of agents and handles a number of products from various insurers. A broker can offer you the widest range of policies to choose from.

INSURANCE COMMISSIONER. State official who regulates insurers and protects the public.

INSURANCE POLICY. A legal contract that sets forth the rights and obligations of both policyholder and insurance company.

INTANGIBLE ASSETS. Long-term assets that lack physical substance, an example is a trademark.

INTEGRATED PENSION PLAN. A pension plan tied in with Social Security so that a participant's monthly pension amount is reduced by a percentage of the monthly Social Security benefit the participant is to receive.

INTEREST. Payments a borrower pays a lender for the use of money. A corporation pays interest on its bonds to its bondholders. Banks pay interest to depositors.

INTEREST ADJUSTED NET COST INDEX. The cost of insurance to the buyer over the life of the insured.

INTEREST EXPENSE. The cost of using borrowed funds.

INTEREST RATE. Rate charged for the use of money.

INTEREST RATE RISK. A systematic risk involving the probability that an investment's value will vary in response to a change in market interest rates.

INTERNATIONAL MUTUAL FUND. A fund that invest in the securities of foreign corporations or governments.

IN-TERROREM. A clause in a will or trust stating that those who contest will forfeit their share.

INTER-VIVOS. Any trust or provision in a trust that becomes effective during the life of the grantor.

INTESTATE. Having made no will; used to identify a situation in which a person dies without a will.

INTRINSIC VALUE OF A SECURITY. The price at which a security should sell under normal market conditions.

INVENTORY. Goods acquired for resale.

INVENTORY TURNOVER RATIO. The cost of goods sold during a period divided by average inventory during that period.

INVESTMENT. An asset held to produce income or appreciate in value.

INVESTMENT BANKING. The industry that specializes in assisting business firms and governments in marketing new security issues.

INVESTMENT FUND. Personal fund set up to accumulate the overflow of the emergency fund. The basis for accumulating retirement income.

INVESTMENT GRADE BONDS. Bonds rated BBB (Standard & Poor's fourth-highest category) and above.

INVESTMENT OBJECTIVE. Goals of investor, such as long-term capital gains, with income secondary.

IRA. See Individual Retirement Arrangement.

IRREVOCABLE LIVING TRUST. A trust that cannot be changed or canceled during your lifetime. It is permanent.

ITEMIZING. Listing all your allowable deductions on Schedule A of Form 1040, as opposed to taking the standard deduction allowed by the IRS.

JOINT AND SURVIVOR ANNUITY. A covered employee designates an individual, usually the spouse, to receive benefits from a pension plan if the worker dies. It provides to the survivor a minimum of 50 percent of the benefit payable to the retiree. To pay for this coverage, the retiree must accept a lower pension while alive.

JOINT RETURN. An individual income tax return filed by a husband and wife together.

JOINT TENANCY. Joint ownership and control over a property or interest during the lifetime of the tenants. Upon the death of a joint tenant, such interest passes automatically to the surviving joint tenant. Property held this way avoids probate but not estate taxes or inheritance taxes.

JOINT VENTURE. Agreement between two or more parties to invest in a piece of property or a business.

JOINT WILL. One will used as the will for two persons and signed by both.

JUNK BONDS. A term used to describe bonds of companies that are in precarious financial straits. They are a very high-risk, high-return investment for speculators who are wiling to gamble. Bonds rated BB or below by Standard & Poor's. Such bonds are riskier than the investment grade bonds.

KEOGH PLAN (HR-10). A tax-deferred retirement plan for self-employed individuals and their employees.

KIDDIE TAX. The requirement that the unearned income over a certain amount of a child under 14 be taxed at the parents' rate.

LATE RETIREMENT. If you reach retirement age, but continue to work, thus delaying the start of your benefits, you receive a bonus, or delayed retirement credit, which increases your social security benefits 3 percent for each year you work.

LEASE. A contract that gives a tenant possession and use of a property under the conditions and terms stated.

LEGACY. A gift of property by will. Also called a bequest.

LETTER OF ADMINISTRATION. A court-issued document in which the person or entity named as administrator of an estate can carry out the prescribed duties.

LETTERS TESTAMENTARY. A court-ordered document in which the person or entity can carry out the prescribed duties as executor under a will.

LEVEL TERM. Term life insurance whereby the benefits remain the same but the premiums increase over time.

LEVERAGE. Accelerative effect of debt on financial returns when buying securities or other assets with borrowed money.

LEVERAGED BUY-OUT (LBO). Process of buying a corporation's stock with borrowed money, then perhaps repaying at least part of the debt from the corporation's assets.

LIABILITIES. All forms of indebtedness for which an individual, a family, or a business is legally liable. What you owe.

LIABILITY COVERAGE. Insurance that protects you against claims by others.

LIFE ANNUITY WITH A TERM CERTAIN. Payment to one person is guaranteed for life with a guarantee period, such as 10 years certain or 20 years certain. If the insured dies before the end of the certain term, a designated beneficiary receives the same monthly income for the remainder of the period.

LIFE ESTATE. The right to beneficial use, but not ownership, of property for a lifetime.

LIFE INSURANCE. Financial protection for one's dependents or beneficiaries against the hardships they would suffer from the loss of the insured if the insured died prematurely.

LIFE INSURANCE TRUST. A frequent element in estate planning. This kind of trust is the beneficiary of a life insurance policy.

LIFE LEASE. The right to occupy property as a tenant for a lifetime.

LIFETIME GIFT. Effective vehicle of transfer in estate planning. Gifts eliminate all probate and administration expenses on the property transferred.

LIMITED LIABILITY. The legal condition which exists when an owner cannot be held personally liable for the debts of an entity beyond the amount that he or she has already invested in the enterprise.

LIMITED PARTNERSHIP. Vehicle for investing in which the investor is a direct owner but has no responsibility for management or liability for the partnership's debts beyond his or her initial investment. The general partner manages the investment.

LIMITED PAYMENT LIFE INSURANCE. Similar to a whole or straight life insurance policy except that premium payments end after a specified number of years, such as 10, 20, or 30 years, or at a specified age. The insured is still covered for life insurance after the premium payments are completed.

LIQUIDITY. Measurement of how readily an investment can be converted into cash.

LIVING TRUST. Created by an individual who is living to be effective during the maker's lifetime. The property is placed in the hands of a trustee to be managed by the trustee for the benefit of one or more individuals. Something to consider for estate planning. Revocable living trusts are used to avoid probate, to avoid having assets on public record, and to reduce the time the assets are frozen.

LIVING WILL. A written request that the life of the individual not be prolonged by artificial means when death is inevitable.

LOAD. Commission charge that buyers of certain mutual funds must pay. The load goes to the stockbroker or the distributor.

LOAD MUTUAL FUND. Type of mutual fund in which the buyer must pay a sales fee or commission on top of the price of the shares. In most cases, no commission is charged when shares are sold. About half of mutual funds are load mutual funds.

LONG-TERM. Generally considered a period longer than one year.

LONG-TERM CARE INSURANCE. Pays for the cost of prolonged stays in a nursing home. It fills the gap left by Medicare, which only picks up the cost for stays at skilled nursing homes after at least three days in a hospital.

LONG-TERM LIABILITIES. Liabilities due after one year.

LOSS RATIO. The amount an insurer pays out in benefits compared to how much it collects in premiums.

LUMP-SUM DISTRIBUTION. An employer's one-time payment of all the balance due to an employee from a pension or profit-sharing plan.

MAJOR MEDICAL COVERAGE. Supplement to basic hospitalization and medical surgical coverage.

MANAGEMENT FEE (Mutual Fund). Money that a mutual fund pays its investment adviser; usually 1/2% to 1% of the fund's net assets.

MARGIN. In securities, the amount of cash down payment and money borrowed from a broker to purchase stocks; in futures, a deposit of money that can be used by the broker to cover losses that may occur in trading futures.

MARGIN ACCOUNT. An investor maintains a deposit of money in a brokerage account. When a stock is bought, only part of the purchase price is cash; the rest is borrowed from the broker. Buying on margin is done in the hope of a price advance, enabling the trader to repay the loan and make a profit. If the market declines, however, the broker may request an additional deposit in the margin account. If it is not forthcoming, the stock is sold to liquidate the loan, and the trader suffers a loss.

MARGINAL TAX BRACKET. The rate at which the last amount of your income is taxed; your highest tax bracket.

MARGIN TRADING. Using borrowed funds for trading.

MARITAL DEDUCTION. Deduction available to the surviving spouse of a decedent. Only the net amount of property that passes to the surviving spouse is allowed as a marital deduction. This deduction is also available to arrive at a value for taxable gifts of property given to a spouse. The current law permits an unlimited marital deduction.

MARITAL DEDUCTION TRUST. Refers to the creation of a trust from which a spouse is entitled to the lifetime income and over which the spouse has enough control to make the corpus includable in his or her gross estate at death.

MARKETABLE SECURITIES. Highly liquid equity securities.

MARKET EFFICIENCY. Description of how prices in competitive markets react to new information.

MARKET RISK. A systematic risk resulting from the tendency of the price of an investment to rise and fall in value in conjunction with the market as a whole.

MARKET TIMING. Attempting to buy securities near the end of a bear market and to sell them near the end of a bull market - in other words, to buy low and sell high.

MATURITY. Date that borrowed money must be paid back.

MAXIMUM FAMILY BENEFIT. There is a limit on the total amount of benefits that all members of one family may receive based on the earnings record of one worker. This limit varies with the primary insurance amount.

MEDICAID. A public assistance program, administered as part of the state or local welfare department, which is designed to provide medical benefits for people of all ages who are unable to pay for health care. Application may be made through the local office of the welfare department.

MEDICAL COVERAGE. Auto insurance that pays for medical expenses of the driver and passengers injured in the insured's vehicle.

MEDICAL SURGICAL COVERAGE. Insurance that pays for treatments by health care professionals.

MEDICARE. A Federal health insurance program for people 65 or older and for certain disabled people which is run by the Health Care Financing Administration and utilizes the services of local Social Security Administration offices. It offers hospitalization and medical care to senior citizens.

MEDICARE AID. An extension of medicare coverage to people under 65 who have been entitled to Social Security disability payments for 24 consecutive months or more, and to people requiring kidney transplants or dialysis treatment.

MEDIGAP INSURANCE. A form of supplemental major medical insurance which covers some or all of the gaps in medicare coverage.

MINIMUM RISK. Safe investments which offer safety of your original investment and may be easily converted to cash.

MISSTATEMENT OF AGE CLAUSE. Allows the insurer to pay the amount of death benefit that the insured would have been allowed had the insured listed his or her correct age.

MODERATE RISK. Semi-safe investments in which many provide regular income and potential long-term growth, but do carry a risk of some loss of the original investment or fluctuations in the rate of return.

MOMENTUM FOLLOWING. Buying funds or stocks that have been excelling and selling those that are faltering.

MONEY MARKET. The collective name for transactions involving the borrowing and lending of money for a short term by the government, banks, large corporations, securities dealers, and individual investors. Short term is considered to be less than one year.

MONEY MARKET DEPOSIT ACCOUNT. Investment vehicle offered by banks to investors to put their money into short-term deposit accounts; usually pays less than money market mutual funds and restricts withdrawals on a monthly basis; federally insured under most circumstances.

MONEY MARKET MUTUAL FUND. A mutual fund that invests in debt obligations with maturities of no more than one year. To keep the principal unchanging, usually at $1 a share, the fund varies the yield. Banks' funds are called money market deposit accounts.

MOODY'S INVESTORS SERVICE. A well-known bond rating service. The highest rating is AAA (Triple A) and the lowest is C. (See Standard & Poor's Corporation).

MORTGAGE-BACKED SECURITIES. Shares of pooled mortgages issued by Fannie Mae (Federal National Mortgage Association), Freddie Mac (Federal Home Loan Mortgage Corporation), or Ginnie Mae (Government National Mortgage Association). Investors receive regular payments of both principal and interest from the underlying mortgages.

MORTGAGEE. A lender in a transaction involving a mortgage instrument.

MORTGAGE INSURANCE. Life insurance designed to pay off a mortgage in the event of the insured's death.

MORTGAGE REIT. Real estate investment trust that concentrates on lending money to builders and buyers of real property.

MORTGAGOR. A borrower or owner in a mortgage transaction who pledges property as security for a debt.

MOVING AVERAGES. Average price of securities over a few days or several years. The general direction of prices is a key guide used by market timers.

MUNICIPAL BOND. Bond issued by a city, state, county, or public agency, the interest from which is typically not taxed by the Federal Government for Federal Income Tax Purposes.

MUNICIPAL BOND FUND. A mutual fund that invests in tax-exempt bonds issued by states, cities and local governments. The bonds may be short, intermediate or long term, and they may be high rated or low rated.

MUTUAL FUND. A company that collects investment money from hundreds or thousands of small investors and manages it for a fee A mutual fund is classified according to its investment objective.

NAKED CALL. Risky option position in which one sells a call option to earn the premium income without owning the underlying security.

NASD (NATIONAL ASSOCIATION OF SECURITIES DEALERS). The group that polices Securities and Exchange Commission rules governing mutual funds and over-the-counter securities.

NASDAQ (NATIONAL ASSOCIATION OF SECURITIES DEALERS AUTOMATED QUOTATIONS). A group that provides price quotations on over-the-counter securities and on mutual funds.

NEGATIVE AMORTIZATION. An arrangement whereby the mortgage payment does not fully cover the interest due, and the difference is then added to the principal owed.

NEGOTIABLE ORDER OF WITHDRAWAL ACCOUNT (NOW ACCOUNT). Checking accounts that earn interest, or viewed another way, savings accounts on which checks can be written.

NET ASSETS. Value of a person's or entity's holdings, minus debts outstanding.

NET ASSET VALUE PER SHARE. A mutual fund's total assets minus its total liabilities divided by the shares outstanding.

NET ESTATE. The value of all of the property wholly or partially owned by an individual at the time of death, after debts and administrative and funeral expenses have been deducted. The net estate is subject to state and federal taxes.

NET INCOME. The difference between the sum of revenues and gains and the sum of expenses and losses.

NET INVESTMENT INCOME. Excess of investment income over investment expense.

NET WORTH. Monetary value of an individual, a family, or a business. It is equal to total assets minus total liabilities.

NO-LOAD MUTUAL FUND. Has no sales force, charges no commission or sales fee, and waits for investors to buy its shares. About one-half of mutual funds are no-load.

NON-CONTRIBUTORY PENSION PLAN. A pension plan financed entirely by the employer. The majority of corporate pension plans are noncontributory.

NON-FORFEITURE CLAUSE. Explains what will happen if you default on paying premiums on a cash value life insurance policy.

NON-MARITAL TRUST. Trust that is created for the purpose of avoiding taxation on the exemption equivalent amount of $600,000.

NON-RECOURSE LOAN. Loans in which the lender has no recourse against the borrower's personal assets in the event of the borrower's default.

NORMAL RETIREMENT BENEFITS. Most pension plans have designed their benefit programs for retirement at age 65, the normal retirement age. While some employees work beyond 65, the Federal law forbidding age discrimination does not require an employer to continue to contribute to the pension plan for individuals who work past the age of 65.

NUNCUPATIVE WILL. Oral will that is generally not held to be valid.

OBLIGOR (Annuity). Party who receives cash or other property from an annuitant in exchange for the unsecured promise to make periodic payments of money to the annuitant for a specific period of time.

OFFERING PRICE (Mutual Funds). Price per share of a mutual fund, plus sales charges.

OLD-AGE, SURVIVORS, AND DISABILITY INSURANCE (OASDI). One of two separate programs in the Social Security structure. The other is the Hospital Insurance program. Each program sets a tax. The two taxes are added together and collected as one amount whether you are an employee or self-employed. The OASDI tax pays for monthly benefits to entitled beneficiaries.

OPEN-END MUTUAL FUND. A fund that can continually issue more shares and thus add to its net assets. It also purchases the shares of those desiring redemption. It buys and sells its shares at a fixed price and uses whatever funds it has for investment.

OPTION. The right to buy or sell investments in the future at certain prices.

ORAL WILL. Made in military combat and within hearing of two witnesses, it is used primarily by soldiers, sailors in active service, or mariners at sea.

OVER-THE-COUNTER. Market in which securities are bought and sold through dealers, not on the floor of an exchange. OTC stocks are typically those of smaller companies.

OWNERS' EQUITY. In accounting, the result of subtracting the liabilities from the assets on a financial statement. Also called shareholders' equity in the case of a corporation.

PART A. Hospital insurance portion of the federal medicare program.

PART B. Medical insurance portion of the federal medicare program.

PARTICIPATING PREFERRED STOCK. A company's stock which is entitled to its stated dividend and also to additional dividends on a specified basis after payment of dividends on the company's common stock.

PARTNERSHIP. Agreement between two or more associates to enter into business or to invest in assets. A partnership is a flow-through entity and pays no federal taxes.

PAR VALUE. As applied to stocks and bonds, the face value printed on the stock certificate or on the bond instrument. Par value is assigned at the time of original issue. Most stocks are issued with no par value.

PASSBOOK SAVINGS ACCOUNT. A form of bank account which pays a relatively low interest rate.

PAY-AS-YOU-GO (Social Security). Almost all of the taxes paid into the Social Security system in a particular year by workers are paid out to that year's Social Security beneficiaries. This system was replaced by a funded pension system after the 1983 Social Security Amendments.

PAYMENT DATE (Mutual Funds). The date when a mutual fund makes distributions. It is usually a few days after the date of record, when distributions are set aside from assets.

PAY-OUT PHASE. The period of time that an annuity is making distributions.

PAY-OUT RATIO. Cash dividends divided by net income.

PAY-OUTS. Distributions from a company's pension or profit-sharing plan.

PENNY STOCKS. Issues selling at less than $5.00 a share. These low-priced issues are often highly speculative and risky.

PENSION BENEFIT GUARANTEE CORPORATION (PBGC). An agency established by the Employee Retirement Income Security Act (ERISA) of 1974 which guarantees benefits to private pension plan members even when a plan's assets are insufficient to fulfill the commitments.

PENSION PLAN BENEFIT. A payment , usually monthly, paid to an individual who has retired from active work and was a member of a pension plan.

PER CAPITA. Means for each person.

PERFORMANCE. How well an investment has done over a certain time period.

PERMANENT INSURANCE. Another name for whole life insurance.

PERSONAL BALANCE SHEET. A report listing the assets, liabilities and new worth of an individual.

PERSONAL FINANCIAL STATEMENTS. Financial reports prepared for an individual which include a personal balance sheet and personal income statement.

PERSONAL INCOME STATEMENT. A report listing revenues and expenditures for an individual usually over a one year period.

PERSONAL PROPERTY. Anything that is not real property or real estate. The two types are tangible personal property, which is something you can touch, such as clothing, a car, a boat; and intangible personal property, which is the ownership of a right or an interest that is protected by law, such as an invention, a stock certificate, or a savings account.

PER STIRPES. The right to an inheritance that exists by virtue of the rights of a deceased ancestor.

PHASED RETIREMENT. A program to help older employees to retire gradually by reducing present work time without reducing ultimate pension benefits.

PINK SHEETS. Daily listings of over-the-counter stocks and their market makers, named for the color of paper used for the lists.

PLURAL OWNERSHIP. Ownership and control of property by more than one person. The different types of ownership are treated differently at death. Also called concurrent ownership.

POINTS. The up front charge from a lending institution for loaning money.

POLICY LOAN. Loan feature available to owner of a cash value life insurance policy.

PONZI SCHEME. A scam in which the first few investors are paid earnings out of the proceeds of later investors.

PORTFOLIO. All the various investments held by an individual or a entity.

PORTFOLIO MANAGER. Person or entity that makes investment decisions for a portfolio.

POUR-OVER WILL. A will that accompanies a living trust and provides that any assets of the decedent that are not held in trust at the time of death pour over into the trust for distribution in accordance with its terms.

POWER OF APPOINTMENT. A power granted by one person to another person to name a beneficiary.

POWER OF ATTORNEY. A document whereby a person or persons give the right to handle all or part of their assets to another to act in their behalf.

PRE-EXISTING CONDITIONS LIMITATION. A limit on coverage allowed for a health condition that one had before becoming insured.

PREFERRED PROVIDER ORGANIZATION (PPO). Panel of health care providers who render services to a group at prearranged fees.

PREFERRED STOCK. Securities entitled to receive fixed and stated dividends before earnings are distributed to the common stockholders. Preferred stock represents an ownership interest in a corporation, usually having the right to vote when preferred dividends are in default for a specified period. In case of bankruptcy or liquidation, preferred stockholders have priority over common stockholders in the division of the company's assets, but only after bondholders have been paid.

PREMIUM. Percentage that a security's price exceeds its net asset or face value per share. A bond that is paying a higher interest rate than the general market may sell for more than its face value and therefore be selling at a premium.

PRENUPTIAL AGREEMENT. Contract between two people who intend to marry. It outlines the intent of both parties relative to the distribution of the property of each at death or divorce.

PREPAYMENT PENALTY. A charge levied by a lender when a mortgage is paid off in part or in full prior to maturity.

PRESENT INTEREST. Unrestricted right to the immediate use, possession or enjoyment of property or the income from property.

PREVAILING CHARGE (Health Insurance). For each covered service and supply, the prevailing charge is the amount which is high enough to cover the customary charges in three out of every four bills submitted to the carrier in the previous year.

PRICE-EARNINGS RATIO (P/E RATIO). Price per share divided the company's earnings per share in the last 12 months. The p/e ratio indicates how popular a stock is by reflecting how much investors are willing to pay for its earning power.

PRIMARY INSURANCE AMOUNT. The largest benefit a worker can receive from Social Security upon retirement.

PRIMARY MARKET. The market for new issues of securities.

PRIME RATE. Interest rate banks charge to their most credit-worthy customers.

PRINCIPAL. The actual loan amount as opposed to interest or income.

PRIVATE ANNUITY. Arrangement in which a transferor transfers property to a transferee in exchange for the transferee's unsecured promise to make periodic payments for the remainder of the transferor's life.

PROBATE. The judicial process of establishing the validity of a will and supervising the distribution of an estate's assets. It has nothing to do with federal estate and/or state inheritance taxes. See probate assets and probate court.

PROBATE ASSETS. The only institution that has the authorization and power by law to change the title of assets owned by a deceased person. The portion of an estate that is subject to probate and thus becomes a matter of public record.

PROBATE COURT. The only institution that has the authorization and power by law to change the title of assets owned by a deceased person. Acts as a referee and decision maker by answering pertinent questions and resolving conflicts of interpretation of a will.

PROFIT-SHARING PLAN. A deferred tax retirement plan , offered by employers, in which the amount of money contributed for the employees benefit may vary from year to year.

PROPERTY. Things or rights that people acquire for the purpose of ownership.

PROPRIETORSHIP. A business with a single owner which has not been incorporated.

PROSPECTUS. Official document describing a mutual fund or other investment.

PURCHASING POWER RISK. A risk resulting from the impact of inflation or deflation on an investment.

PUT OPTION. A right to sell a fixed number of shares of stock at a specified price within a limited period of time. The purchaser hopes that the stock's price will go down by an amount sufficient to provide a profit when the option is sold. If the stock price remains the same or goes up, the investment in the put option is lost.

QUALIFIED PENSION PLAN. One which meets a set of specified criteria, developed by the Internal Revenue Service, that enables the employer to deduct contributions to the plan from taxable income as a business expense and allows earnings to accumulate tax free until distribution. Also called qualified retirement plan.

QUALIFIED TERMINABLE INTEREST PROPERTY (QTIP) TRUST. A trust that allows a person to provide income to a surviving spouse, but upon his/her death the assets go to whomever the grantor (original spouse) chooses.

QUARTERLY FINANCIAL STATEMENTS. Financial statements issued every three months.

QUARTERS OF COVERAGE (QC) (Social Security). A minimum number of calendar quarters of coverage is required in order to be fully insured, that is, eligible for the various types of Social Security benefits.

RANDOM WALK. The theory that stock prices are unpredictable.

RATE OF RETURN. The amount of annual interest, dividends or cash flow from an investment divided by the initial cost.

RATIO ANALYSIS. A method of expressing financial statement relationships.

RATIO OF RETURN ON ASSETS. Net income divided by total assets.

REAL ESTATE BROKER. A licensed professional the specializes in the sale and leasing of real estate property.

REAL ESTATE INVESTMENT TRUST (REIT). Similar to a mutual fund. Small investors buy shares in a REIT that invests in real estate, including apartments, shopping centers and large commercial properties. Because of the nature of the real estate market, a REIT is highly speculative and is risky but is more liquid than owning the real estate directly.

REAL PROPERTY. Includes land and the buildings on it. It is referred to as real estate as opposed to personal property.

RECOURSE LOAN. The lender has recourse against the borrower's personal assets (subject to local statutes) in the event of the borrower defaulting on the loan.

REDEMPTION FEE. The charge a mutual fund levies if shares are sold before a specified date. Sometimes referred to as a back-end fee.

REGISTERED BOND. Registered on the books of the issuing company or governmental unit in the name of the owner whose name also appears on the bond. A registered bond can be transferred only when endorsed by the registered owner.

REINSTATEMENT CLAUSE. Allows the insured to revive a policy that has lapsed or been discontinued for nonpayment of premiums.

RELEASE. Agreement that an insured will not seek additional payments from the insurer as a result of an incident.

RENEWABLE TERM INSURANCE. Term life insurance that can be renewed without proof of insurability.

RENUNCIATION. Giving up a gift or a bequest, usually for post mortem tax-planning purposes.

REPLACEMENT COST COVERAGE HOMEOWNERS INSURANCE. Insurance coverage for a house and/or contents to restore the loss to its original state of workmanship and materials.

REPLACEMENT VALUE. The cost to replace in as new condition a damaged building or other property.

REPORTABLE TRANSACTION. A transaction you must list on your tax return.

REPURCHASE AGREEMENT. Known as a repo. A bank in need of money for a short period of time, usually one or more days, borrows money from a money market fund, using U.S. Treasury securities as collateral. The bank sells Treasury paper to the money market fund with the provision that it will buy the paper back within the specified period of time. This transaction is documented through a repo agreement.

RESIDUARY ESTATE. Property left in an estate after payment of costs, debts and specific bequests.

RETAINED EARNINGS. The earnings of the corporation that have been retained for use in the business rather than distributed to the shareholders as dividends.

RETIREMENT PLANNING. A process that involves saving and investing for your retirement years, protecting yourself from financial disaster and becoming an educated financial consumer.

RETURN ON EQUITY (ROE). Net income divided by owners' or stockholders' equity.

REVENUE BOND. A municipal bond whose payment of interest and repayment of principal are backed by the income earned by the facility, such as an airport, bridge, or tunnel, built with the money raised by the bond issue.

REVERSE ANNUITY MORTGAGE. Arrangement whereby an older homeowner receives regular payments from a lender in return for the lender eventually having rights to sell the home and be reimbursed for the payments made to the homeowner.

REVERSE MORTGAGE. Enables retirees to cash in on the increased value of their homes by borrowing against the increased value, taking money out in a lump-sum and investing in an annuity, yielding regular monthly income.

REVOCABLE. A condition that permits amending or nullifying at will, for example, the grantor can change or even terminate a revocable trust.

REVOCABLE LIVING TRUST. A trust that can be changed or canceled during the lifetime of the grantor.

RIDER. An added coverage to the basic insurance policy.

RIGHT OF SURVIVORSHIP. The right of a joint tenant to take property in its entirety when the other joint owner is deceased.

RISK. Possibility that investors will lose all or part of their money.

RISK MANAGEMENT. Identification and measurement of risk exposures and decisions on how to handle the identified risks.

RISK TOLERANCE. Ability of a person to accept what may be temporary or permanent losses from an investment.

ROLLOVER. The tax-free transfer of a distribution from a qualified retirement plan to another qualified retirement plan within 60 days.

ROUND LOTS. Stocks sold in groups of 100 shares.

SALARY REDUCTION PLAN. Known as a 401(k) plan or a 403(b) plan, a salary reduction plan allows employees to earmark a portion of their salary for deposit into the plan. Income taxes are deferred until the money is withdrawn, usually at retirement.

SALES CHARGE. Commission an investor must pay to buy certain investments.

SALES CONTRACT. An agreement between two or more parties, containing the terms and conditions of the sale. The contract must be written and signed by both parties.

SAVINGS BOND. A security sold by the U.S. government that offers fixed income with minimum risk and minimum investment. The bonds are sold at a discount and the interest accumulates over a designated time period. Also used for college savings plans.

SCHEDULE C. The tax form schedule used by self-employed persons. Lists business income less expenses.

S CORPORATION. A corporation with 35 or fewer shareholders that elects not to be taxed like a regular corporation. The corporate income and expenses flow through to the shareholders based upon their ownership interests.

SECONDARY MARKET. The market where securities are bought and sold subsequent to original issuance.

SECOND MORTGAGE. A loan that uses as security a piece of property that is already security for a first mortgage loan.

SECTOR. Stocks in one industry.

SECTOR FUND. A mutual fund which invest in one industry or segment of the economy (e.g. financial services).

SECULAR. Long-term.

SECURITIES. Stock, bonds, options, warrants or other instruments, that signify a financial obligation to an investor.

SECURITIES AND EXCHANGE COMMISSION. U.S. government agency that administers the federal laws that protect an investor of publicly traded securities.

SELF-EMPLOYMENT CONTRIBUTIONS ACT. The Federal law that sets the tax rate and the maximum taxable amount for the self-employed. An amendment to this law can change the tax rate and/or the maximum taxable amount. This is similar to the FICA tax paid by employees and their employers.

SERIES FUND. A mutual fund with more than one portfolio.

SETTLEMENT OPTION. Method of payment when life insurance pays off.

SETTLOR. Person in a trust relationship who creates or intentionally causes the trust to come into existence. Also called donor, trustor and grantor.

SHAREHOLDERS OR STOCKHOLDERS EQUITY. The summation of a corporation's contributed capital and retained earnings. It comprises the corporate assets minus the corporate liabilities.

SHORT-TERM. Generally a period less than one year.

SHORT SALE. Sale of a security which is not owned with the intention of purchasing it later at a lower price. Short sellers expect a security's price to decline.

SIGNATURE GUARANTEE. Document in which an investor's signature is warranted as authentic. Signature guarantees may be required before a shareholder can redeem mutual fund shares. The guarantee usually must be made by a commercial bank or national brokerage firm, not by a notary.

SIMPLIFIED EMPLOYEE PENSION (SEP). A qualified retirement plan for the self-employed.

SIMULTANEOUS DEATH. The death of the testator or grantor and a beneficiary under circumstances in which it cannot be determined who died first.

SINGLE PREMIUM ANNUITY. An annuity purchased with a single lump-sum payment.

SINGLE PREMIUM WHOLE LIFE. A form of cash value life insurance in which the insured makes a single premium payment. No further payments are required.

SMALL BUSINESS ADMINISTRATION (SBA). A U.S. government agency created in 1953 to aid small business concerns by providing financial, technical, and managerial assistance.

SOCIAL SECURITY. A Federal program established in 1935 to provide retirement, survivors' benefits, disability, and medical benefits through a payroll tax paid both by employers and employees and self-employed individuals.

SOCIAL SECURITY ADMINISTRATION (SSA). The Social Security Administration administers the Old Age, Survivors, and Disability Insurance (OASDI) programs.

SOLE OWNERSHIP. Ownership and control of property by own person who, upon death, leaves it to chosen heirs.

SPECIAL AGENT. A member of the Criminal Investigation Division of the IRS, the sole objective of which is to develop a criminal case against taxpayers.

SPECIALIST. Member of a stock exchange who is obligated to make a fair and orderly market in one or more securities.

SPECIALIZED MUTUAL FUND. A mutual fund which concentrates its investments in one or two fields, such as a specific industry, precious metals, commodities, options, foreign stocks, and so forth.

SPECIAL PURPOSE FUND. Personal fund to accumulate savings for special purposes. This fund could be used for education for your children, care for family members, reduction of debt or vacations.

SPECIAL SITUATION. Stock that is expected to benefit from a new development, such as an important new product or management change.

SPENDTHRIFT CLAUSE. A clause in a will or trust stating that a creditor cannot collect on the future interest of a beneficiary.

SPREAD. Difference between the asking price and the bid price for an investment, like a stock or bond.

SPRINKLING PROVISION. Provision that is established to allow the trustee to invade the corpus for the surviving spouse or for the remainder person.

SPRINKLING TRUST. The trustee has the power to make distributions according to a standard such as need rather than according to a preset percentage. This gives a trustee the power to distribute income, and possibly principal, according to the needs of each beneficiary.

STANDARD & POOR'S CORPORATION. A well-known stock and bond rating service. The highest rating is AAA (Triple A), and the lowest, D. (See Moody's Investors Service.)

STANDARD & POOR'S 500. Popular replica of the stock market as a whole, based on the prices of 500 widely held common stocks.

STANDARD DEDUCTION. A sum you can subtract from your adjusted gross income if you do not itemize all your allowable deductions on Schedule A of Form 1040.

STANDARD DEVIATION. Number representing the volatility of an investment over a period of time. Used to measure the investment's risk. The greater the standard deviation, the greater the variability and the greater the total investment risk.

STATEMENT OF CASH FLOW. Financial statement that shows cash receipts and cash payments over a period of time.

STATUE OF LIMITATIONS. Time limit for initiating a lawsuit.

STEPPED-UP BASIS. The circumstance in which the value of a beneficiary's bequest is increased to the level of its value at the time of the decedent's date of death or a short time thereafter.

STOCK. Basic form of ownership interest in a corporation, this may be in the form of common or preferred stock.

STOCK BROKER. A licensed professional who is registered with the Securities and Exchange Commission to sell securities.

STOCK DIVIDEND. Payment of a corporate dividend in the form of additional shares of common stock.

STOCK SPLIT. An increase in the number of outstanding shares accompanied by a proportionate decrease in the par or stated value.

STRAIGHT BANKRUPTCY. If the debts of an individual are greater than the ability to repay, a

bankruptcy court orders the liquidation of a specified amount of an individual's assets to repay as much of the debts as possible.

STRAIGHT LIFE ANNUITY. Guarantees a stipulated monthly income for one person for life, but ends with that person's death, making no payments to beneficiaries or survivors. It has no cash surrender value. May be appropriate for individuals who have no dependents and want maximum income.

STRIPS. A zero coupon bond issued by the U.S. government with separate trading of the interest and principal portions of securities.

STUDENTS' BENEFITS. A Social Security program which provides monthly payments to full-time students between ages 18 and 22 because of the death, disability, or retirement of a parent who worked long enough under Social Security.

SUCCESSOR. One named in a will or trust to replace a trustee or executor who cannot serve.

SUCCESSOR GUARDIAN. An additional guardian listed in a will, who can assume the responsibilities of guardian in case your initial guardian dies or is otherwise unable to perform the functions.

SUICIDE CLAUSE. States that the company will not pay a death benefit if the insured commits suicide within two years after the policy is purchased.

SUMMARY PLAN DESCRIPTION (SPD). A summary description of a pension plan that the Employee Retirement Income Security Act of 1974 requires be given to each employee covered by the plan. It must include information on eligibility requirements for benefits, accumulation of benefits, loss of benefits, termination insurance, and the method for filing a claim for benefits.

SUPER NOW ACCOUNT. The Super Negotiable order of Withdrawal Account (Super NOW Account) pays an interest rate that is higher than the NOW account but somewhat less than a Money Market Deposit Account, requires a minimum balance, but offers checking privileges. If an account falls below the minimum balance, the bank applies a penalty fee. These accounts are insured up to $100,000 each and place no limit on the amount of the check written as long as the required minimum balance is maintained.

SUPPLEMENTAL LETTER OF INSTRUCTIONS. A memorandum of personal details that should be attached to your will with a copy to your executor and one for you and your spouse so that it may be kept up-to-date. The Supplemental Letter of Instructions should include such information as location of the will, location of vital documents, location of assets, employment or business information, and funeral and burial instructions.

SUPPLEMENTAL SECURITY INCOME (SSI). A separate Social Security program that provides a basic cash income for people in financial need who are 65 or older, and for the needy of any age who are blind or disabled.

SUPPORT. Payments you make to take care of a dependent, as for shelter and food.

SUPPORT TRUST. Trust that is designed to provide support for the beneficiary.

SURPLUS. The amount by which income exceeds expenditures.

SURROGATE. A judge of the surrogate court who is charged with acting according to the wishes of the decedent.

SURVIVORS' INSURANCE. A Social Security Benefit which is a form of life insurance that provides income to your dependent spouse, your dependent children, and your dependent parents (if they are 62 and over) in the event of your death.

SYSTEMATIC RISK. Investment risk that results from economic, political and sociological factors, include market changes, interest rate fluctuations and purchasing power risks.

TANGIBLE ASSETS. Assets that have a physical substance.

TAXABLE ESTATE. That part of the gross estate that is subject to federal taxes, generally after marital and charitable deductions have been applied.

TAXABLE INCOME. Your income after subtracting adjustments, deductions and exemptions from your gross income.

TAX AVOIDANCE Tax reduction methods permitted by law. See tax evasion.

TAX-DEFERRED. The ability of some investments to allow earnings not to be taxed until a later time.

TAX-DEFERRED ANNUITY. Payments to an annuity account are made with pre-tax dollars, which become tax-sheltered. The insured pays no income taxes on the amount deposited in the annuity account or on the interest earned by the principal. When the insured eventually begins to withdraw the money after retirement, he or she pays income taxes on the amounts withdraw.

TAX EVASION. Any method of reducing taxes not permitted by law, which carries heavy penalties. Involves deceit, subterfuge, camouflage, concealment or an attempt to color or obscure events. See tax avoidance.

TAX-FREE EXEMPTION. The first $600,000 of your gross estate less any marital or charitable

deductions.

TAX RATE (FICA). The percentage of your earnings which are paid by you and your employer each year into the Social Security program. A self-employed individual pays a higher rate. Tax rates are set by Congress.

TAX SHELTER. An investment that produces after-tax income that is greater than before-tax income. These investment vehicles either defer federal taxation, like retirement plans, or escape it altogether, like the interest from municipal bonds. Such investments may provide before-tax cash flow that generate losses to shelter other income from taxation.

TAX-SHELTER ANNUITY. Known as a 401(k) plan or a 403(b) plan, this is a salary reduction plan which allows employees to earmark a portion of their salary for deposit into the plan. Income taxes are deferred until the money is withdrawn, usually at retirement.

TECHNICAL ANALYSIS. Process of predicting future stock price movements by analyzing the historical movement of stock prices and supply and demand forces that affect those prices.

TENANCY BY THE ENTIRETY. A form of property ownership by married couples whereby upon death one spouse's interest is automatically transferred to the other spouse. You may not sell or give away your share without obtaining permission from your spouse.

TENANCY IN COMMON. Each individual of the tenancy owns a specified percentage of the property but not a specific piece. In this form of joint ownership, there is no right of survivorship or automatic transfer at death. The portion owned by each person may be sold, given away, used as collateral, or passed through the particular owner's will.

TERMINABLE INTEREST. Interest that will fail with the passage of time or with the occurrence of an event or contingency. Such an interest is normally ineligible for estate tax marital deduction.

TERM LIFE INSURANCE. Covers the insured for a specified number of years, usually one, five, or ten years, paying the beneficiaries the face amount of the policy if the insured dies within the specified period. The premium is less than a whole life or endowment policy because it accumulates no cash value and represents the cost of pure insurance plus a charge for administration.

TESTAMENTARY. Any provision found in a will or trust that takes effect at death.

TESTATE. One who dies leaving a valid will.

TESTATOR (TESTATRIX, IF A WOMAN). The person who makes a will.

THREE Cs OF CREDIT. In evaluating a borrower, creditors use Three Cs: Capacity, sufficient income to enable a borrower to repay the loan; Character, traits making up an individual's nature that would make the borrower want to repay the loan; and Collateral, sufficient assets of the borrower to fully protect repayment of the loan.

THREE-PART WILL. Will in which some assets pass directly to the spouse, some property goes into a bypass trust, and the remaining property passes to a qualified terminable interest property trust.

TIGRS. A zero coupon bond issued by the U.S. government called Treasury Investment Growth Receipts.

TITLE. A document indicating the legal right by the owner of record to the possession of some real property. Title may be acquired through purchase, inheritance, gift, or foreclosure of a mortgage.

TITLE INSURANCE. Designed to protect owners and lenders against loss from defects in the title.

TITLE SEARCH. The examination of all public records to disclose all facts pertinent to the title of the property.

TOP DOWN. Method of investing in which the investor looks at general economic trends, then decides which industries and companies will benefit.

TOTAL RATE OF RETURN. The interest, dividends or cash flow from an investment plus the capital gains or losses divided by the value of the investment at the beginning of the period.

TOTAL RETURN. Profit or loss that an investment has achieved over a period of time, including capital gains or losses, interest and dividends and expenses. It is expressed as a percentage of the original value of the investment.

TOTTEN TRUST. A bank account that is payable to a named beneficiary upon the death of the depositor. The trust is revocable and is used in place of a will.

TRANSFER. A shift of pension money directly from one custodian to another.

TREASURY SECURITIES. Debt obligations issued by the U.S. government and backed by the faith and credit of that government.

TREASURY STOCK. The repurchase by a company of its own outstanding stock.

TRUST. A legal entity created by the owner of property for the purpose of administering and distributing such property for the benefit of the owner and/or other persons.

TRUSTEE. The person or entity named to act as the fiduciary of the trust and to whom the grantor transfers legal title to the trust property for the benefit of another.

TRUST PROPERTY. Interest in a thing - real or personal, tangible or intangible - that the trustee holds, subject to the rights of another.

TURNOVER RATIO. Trading activity of a mutual fund, calculated by dividing the lesser of purchases or sales for the fund's fiscal year by the monthly average of the portfolio's net assets. Excluded are securities that mature within a year. A turnover ratio of 100% is the equivalent of a complete portfolio turnover.

12b-1 FEES. Fees that a mutual fund is permitted to take out of assets to pay for marketing costs. Usually .25% to 1.25% of assets. Also called a hidden load.

TWO-PART WILL. Will in which some assets pass directly to the surviving spouse while the remaining assets are deposited in a bypass trust.

UMBRELLA COVERAGE. Liability insurance that pays for catastrophic claims beyond the limits of normal personal insurance coverage.

UNDER-FUNDED PENSION PLAN. Exists when a company's pension reserves to meet future pension benefits are inadequate.

UNDERINSURED MOTORIST COVERAGE. First party auto insurance that reimburses the insured if another motorist's insurance coverage is inadequate.

UNEARNED INCOME. Income derived from investments not for work performed.

UNIFIED TAX CREDIT. The amount that can be deducted from the gross estate tax. This deduction is applied against both estate and gift taxes due the government, thus shielding both transfers from taxation. This tax credit is a direct reduction of the total taxes due, saving the taxpayer thousands of dollars. It is the equivalent of the tax on the first $600,000 of the estate valuation.

UNIFORM GIFTS TO MINORS ACT. The law that has been adopted by all fifty states, which permits an adult to make a monetary gift in trust to a minor.

UNINSURED MOTORIST COVERAGE. First party auto insurance that reimburses the insured if another motorist is uninsured.

UNIT INVESTMENT TRUST. Type of mutual fund, typically a diversified portfolio of bonds, in which the bonds are bought and then held to maturity. Shareholders receive interest regularly, and - when the bonds in the trust mature - receive their principal.

UNIVERSAL LIFE INSURANCE. A form of life insurance that enables the policy holder to vary both the amount of premium payment and the amount of death benefit to fit the changing needs of a growing family. Cash values can grow at competitive interest rates, giving the insured some control over the speed of cash buildup.

UNLIMITED LIABILITY. The owners of an individual proprietorship or a partnership are personally responsible for the debts of the business to the full extent of their assets and personal wealth.

UNLIMITED MARITAL DEDUCTION. Under present law, no limit exists on the size of the estate that one spouse can leave for the other, and the transfer is free of estate taxes.

UNSYSTEMATIC RISK. Risk associated with the nature of a business enterprise underlying the investment, which includes business and financial risk.

U.S. TREASURY BILL. Known as T-bills, these short-term securities, maturing in 3, 6, or 12 months, are backed by the full faith and credit of the U.S. government. The T-bill pays an attractive yield that is exempt from state and local income taxes, subject only to Federal income taxes. It is sold at a discount from its $10,000 face value.

U.S. TREASURY BOND. A security that matures in ten or more years, selling at face value, and paying a fixed rate of interest twice a year throughout ownership. Backed by the full faith and credit of the U.S. government, the interest is exempt from state and local income taxes, subject only to Federal income taxes.

U.S. TREASURY NOTE. A security that matures in two to ten years. Backed by the full faith and credit of the U.S. government, the interest is exempt from state and local income taxes, subject only to Federal income taxes.

VARIABLE ANNUITY. The monthly payment fluctuates because the funds in the annuity account are invested in a portfolio of stocks, and stock prices fluctuate daily. If average stock prices rise, the insured receives a higher annuity, and vice versa.

VARIABLE LIFE INSURANCE. A form of life insurance that has a fixed premium similar to a whole life insurance contract but which enables the insured to direct the investment of the cash accumulation among a variety of mutual funds and other types of investments, while providing a guaranteed minimum death benefit.

VARIABLE PREMIUM ANNUITY. An annuity purchased by monthly or annual installment payments, the size of which may be changed at the insured's discretion.

VARIABLE-RATE ANNUITY. Annuity that provides possible high yields because investments are chosen as often as once a month. See annuity and fixed-rate annuity.

VARIABLE UNIVERSAL LIFE. Whole life where you can choose the level of the premium depending on how much money you want contributed to the cash value of the policy, like universal life insurance but just like variable life insurance you direct the investment of the cash accumulation among a variety of investments.

VERY HIGH RISK. Investments where you have a chance to make a lot of money but your chances of losing all or a major portion of your original investment are extremely high, similar to gambling.

VESTING. The absolute right of an employee to receive money from a retirement plan even if he or she resigns or is fired. Employees' contributions vest immediately and can be withdrawn when the employee leaves the job. The rights of employees to employer contributions are generally subject to limitations, including service time requirements.

VOLATILITY. Fluctuations in the price of a security or index of securities.

WAGE EARNER'S PLAN BANKRUPTCY. If the debts of an individual are greater than his or her ability to repay, a bankruptcy court allows an individual to retain his or her property, but requires the individual to set up a court-approved monthly budget plan in order to repay as much of the debts as possible within a three-year period.

WAITING PERIOD. Time that must elapse before disability insurance pays to replace lost income.

WARD. A person incapable of managing personal affairs and for whom a court appoints a conservator.

WHOLE OR STRAIGHT, LIFE INSURANCE. As long as the insured pays the premiums, he or she is insured for life. It includes a savings feature, or cash value, against which the insured can borrow, paying interest on the loan. The insured can withdraw the cash value completely if he or she terminates the life insurance. When he or she dies, the beneficiaries collect the face value of the policy.

WIDOWERS' BENEFITS. A Social Security program that provides monthly benefits to a father if his wife died while insured under Social Security, and if he has not remarried and cares for an unmarried child under 18, or an older child who was disabled before age 22.

WILL. Legal document that serves as a key vehicle of property transfer at death. Within the document are specific instructions concerning the disposition of the estate and naming the designated executor (executrix).

WILL CONTEST. A challenge to a will, often initiated by disgruntled family members. The will in question has usually been made just prior to the death of the maker.

WILSHIRE 5000. Model of all stocks, including those on the New York Stock Exchange, The American Exchange and over-the-counter. The Wilshire is one of the broadest indexes and includes over 6,000 stocks.

WITHHOLDING. Taking taxes from your salary to pay federal and state taxes.

WORKERS' COMPENSATION. A form of disability insurance benefits paid to workers for job related injuries, accidents, and illnesses. It is a source of retirement income for individuals with job-related disabilities.

WORKING CAPITAL. The excess of total current assets over current liabilities.

WRAPAROUND ANNUITY. Enables the owner of the annuity to control the investment of the funds in the account. The owner can invest in stocks or bonds or in a money market mutual fund or any other type of mutual fund, and can switch from one form of investment to another to take advantage of changing market conditions.

YIELD. Regular income from a fund, expressed as a percentage of the fund's average net asset value, not including capital gains or losses.

YIELD CURVE. Graph depicting the relationship between term to maturity and yield to maturity for comparable bonds at a given time. Usually long-term rates are higher than short term rates. When short term rates are higher, it is a negative yield curve.

YIELD TO MATURITY. Concept used to determine the rate of return an investor will receive if a bond is held to its maturity date.

ZERO-COUPON BOND. A bond - corporate, federal or municipal - sold at a small fraction of its face value. It gradually appreciates whereby the yearly interest payments are added to the principal and you receive one large sum at maturity. The "phantom" payments will be taxable every year, except in the case of federal or municipal zeros. An example are U.S. Savings Bonds - Series EE.

RATING AND SUGGESTION FORM

YOUR PERSONAL SURVIVAL GUIDE
ON
PROTECTION

To constantly improve, update and bring you the best educational seminars, we need your assistance and comments. Please fill out this form and mail it back to us at the address given below.

1. My rating of the seminar video tape is:
   _____ Excellent
   _____ Very good
   _____ Average
   _____ Poor

   Why: ____

   ____

   ____

2. My rating of the seminar notebook is:
   _____ Excellent
   _____ Very good
   _____ Average
   _____ Poor

   Why: ____

   ____

   ____

3. My suggestion for additional seminar topics are:

   ____

   ____

   ____

4. I think the video and notebook format could be improved by:

   ____

   ____

   ____

RATING AND SUGGESTION FORM

YOUR PERSONAL SURVIVAL GUIDE
ON
PROTECTION

(continued)

5. Please send your brochure to the following people because I think the material would be beneficial to them:

NAME ______________________ NAME ______________________

ADDRESS ___________________ ADDRESS ___________________

__________________________ __________________________

NAME ______________________ NAME ______________________

ADDRESS ___________________ ADDRESS ___________________

__________________________ __________________________

NAME ______________________ NAME ______________________

ADDRESS ___________________ ADDRESS ___________________

__________________________ __________________________

Please mail to:

SUCCESSFUL RETIREMENT PLANNING INSTITUTE
50 NORTH BROCKWAY - SUITE 4-1
PALATINE, ILLINOIS 60067-5076

Your name and address (optional):

NAME ______________________

ADDRESS ___________________

____

SEMINAR NOTES

SEMINAR NOTES

SEMINAR NOTES